Beth,

Thank you for All you do for me and for All you do for me

May God Bless you As you Read Book!. Pastor [signature]

SHOT IN THE DARK

Hardcover ISBN: 978-1-0880-4477-3
Paperback ISBN: 978-1-9555-4617-1

A Publication of *Tall Pine Books*
119 E Center Street, Suite B4A | Warsaw, Indiana 46580
www.tallpinebooks.com

| 1 22 22 20 16 02 |

Published in the United States of America

SHOT

ONE MAN'S STORY

IN THE

OF SURRENDER AND SURVIVAL

DARK

CHRIS McRAE

"Pastor Chris is a man I have known and respected for many years. I met him for the first time when he was a high school football player, and the Lord spoke clearly to me that he would be in ministry one day. Chris thought his future was football, but the Lord had even greater plans for his life. That's why I love his new book, *Shot in the Dark*.

In it, he shares personal stories along with biblical illustrations that show how God has great plans for our lives. He is always faithful, even when we can't see it. I know the Lord will minister to you through this book."

—ROBERT MORRIS
Senior Pastor, *Gateway Church*
Bestselling Author of *The Blessed Life, Beyond Blessed*,
and *Take the Day Off*

"I met Pastor Chris McRae several years ago at a luncheon for First Liberty Institute, the nation's largest legal organization dedicated to defending religious liberty. I have been thoroughly impressed with the resolve, resiliency, and dedication to biblical citizenship by Pastor Chris. His book *Shot in the Dark* is a must read for men and women of faith, and especially for those needing a story of personal triumph. I have always said that God does not call the equipped, but rather He equips those that He calls.

That premise is certainly true in the life of Pastor Chris McRae, a dynamic man of God. Pastor Chris' book reminds us of Proverbs 3:5-6 and Jeremiah 29:11, and implores us to let go and let God! I have led men in combat, and as a member of *Sojourn Church*, I can attest that Pastor Chris McRae is a godly leader of impeccable, uncompromising, and faith-based principle. *Shot in the Dark* enables the reader to see how it all came to be."

—LIEUTENANT COLONEL ALLEN B. WEST
(US Army, Retired) Member, 112th US Congress
Former Chairman, Republican Party of Texas

"Some life stories are laced with a level of darkness darker than the average, a light a bit brighter, and an outcome that gives God more glory. From a gunshot to a glorious testimony, Pastor Christopher McRae's is just such a sojourn."

—DR. MARK RUTLAND
Executive Director, *The National Institute of Christian Leadership*

"Chris' story is an incredible testament to the love, faithfulness, and goodness of our God. Chris is an overcomer and has gone through situations and circumstances that most of us couldn't even dream of, but he has seen God's hand in the midst of some of the most difficult moments this life can offer.

His story will challenge, convict, and encourage you. Regardless of your current situation, Chris' testimony will remind you to keep your eyes on Jesus and trust in Him."

—TIM BARTON
President, *WallBuilders*

"Chris McRae is an amazing example of perseverance and how faithfulness and humility results in promotion. Even though he is an extraordinarily gifted person and communicator—through the years he was always willing to serve -willing to stand in the gap and help at any level of need. This book will inspire every person to be a committed Christ follower and to believe God for great things in their life. I highly endorse it!"

—BISHOP JOSEPH MATTERA

Author, USCAL Convener, *Mattera Ministries International*

"Chris McRae has such a powerful life testimony of God's goodness, love and sustaining power. His life journey is a strong statement of God's goodness and passion towards us. He is a very gifted pastor, storyteller and has a refreshing sense of humor. Don't miss out, there's an encounter awaiting for you as you read!"

—ROBBY DAWKINS

Bestselling Author, Speaker, Equipper

"The amazing story God is telling through the life of Chris McRae is not only intriguing and captivating, in the telling, but grace-glorifying in its influence. I've been privileged to share in in much of this journey. I'm convinced that Chris is a voice that will be increasingly be heard and respected among those called to make a positive difference in this time."

—DUDLEY HALL

President, *Kerygma Ventures*

"Pastor Chris McRae is an amazing example of the kind of God-fearing, champion of a man that we need in society today. His life experiences and heavenly insights should give us all hope, and much-needed inspiration for the times we are living in. This book, is one that is sure to inspire, challenge, and fuel us with courage to be the best version of ourselves. I'm honored to know him as a brother."

—DAVID HARRIS JR.
CEO, *DJHJ Media*

CONTENTS

Foreword 11

Introduction: A Note on Community 13

1. Starting Early 17
2. Turning Tides 25
3. Coming of Age 35
4. Destination Dallas 43
5. Bible School 51
6. Journey to Sojourn 63
7. Offspring and Opportunities 71
8. The Shot 81
9. The Rushed Ride 91
10. Under the Knife 103
11. Finding Normal 115
12. The Temple Victory 127
13. Lesions and Lessons 133
14. Messages from the Mess 147
15. The Fallout and the Future 163

Afterword: A Note on Trauma 179
Author Bio 185
Endnotes 187

BY TERRY MOORE

FOREWORD

When a young African American man showed up nearly 25 years ago to the church on Sojourn Drive, I asked the same question I do whenever I meet anyone: *Lord, what do You have for this young man? And, How can I be Your heart extended so that he can be all You've called him to be?* Little did either of us know what God had in store. From having a casual acquaintance with Chris, to establishing a mentorship, to becoming one of my spiritual sons, we've grown in our relationship with the Lord and our appreciation for each other's unique calling.

I've read the miracles in the Bible, I've heard people share testimonies of the amazing things they've seen God do, but I can truly say that night was one of the darkest of my life. Every fiber of my faith in a miracle working God was put to the test and He did not fail. Jesus tells us in John 10:10, "The thief does not come except to steal, kill, and to destroy. I have come that they may have life, and that they may have it more abundantly." As you read this book, I hope you will see the goodness of God in miraculous ways.

I believe you will be challenged as you hear the truth of who God is and His eternal and unconditional love for you and the power that is available to those who believe in Jesus. If you don't have a relationship with Jesus, it is my prayer that you become introduced to Him and accept Him as your personal Savior.

Walking with my friend and spiritual son, Chris, through the transitions from being a young man with a desire for preaching to a mature senior pastor with a heart to make a difference and advance God's kingdom on earth, has been eventful, exciting, and continually covered by grace. In a forthcoming volume, we will unpack these transitions and successions in more detail, but for now, I encourage you to read with an open heart, ready to receive both inspiration and insight.

—Terry Moore
Founding Pastor, *Sojourn Church*

A NOTE ON COMMUNITY

A filthy-rich business tycoon was living on the out-skirts of a small town in Midwest America. It was the 1950s. He had made his millions but had made no friends along the way. He was bitter, angry, depressed, and resented humanity as a whole. Even his property looked down on people, as his giant mansion over-looked the town beneath it.

As an old man, any relatives he had were long dead. He had no family of his own and no tight relationships to speak of. In fact, the only person he saw somewhat regularly was his stockbroker.

As he grew older, he knew death was near. Angry at God, angry at the world, and deep down, angry with himself—he drew up a will. Following his death, the judge in probate court was astonished when he reviewed the will. It stated, "I leave my property and my entire estate to the devil."

The judge did not exactly have Lucifer on speed dial to fill him in on his new inheritance. He decided to think on the issue for several days. After some time, he came back to court and said, "I have a solution. I order that a massive, impenetrable fence be installed to surround this property so that nothing can get out and nothing can get in."

Those in the courtroom scratched their heads. He continued, "The property will be totally isolated. Because anything that is left to itself, cut off from anyone or anything else, by default, winds up in the hands of the devil."

My story is one of being brought from internal isolation into genuine, life-giving community. The enemy owns all of the isolated real estate in our lives, so to speak. For many of my formative years, my default switch was isolation. I may have been surrounded by folks on the outside but was alone on the inside. Yet as God had His way, the years passed and circumstances shifted, and God found me, and *I found me*, as a result.

Had I not been plugged into vibrant communities of healthy believers at varying stages of my life, God only knows where I would be today. Given the events of my story, six feet under seems likely. From peaks to valleys, I've seen the unmatched faithfulness of God and the genuine compassion of His people.

A healthy church community is like an IV in the arms of those who attend. In medical terms, *intravenous* is a means of administering medicine to a patient directly into the vein. God utilizes the church like an IV, to deliver hope, encouragement, inspiration, and *life* into the members. If we are isolated, blocked off, and hidden away, we pull the IV out of our arm, so to speak, and forgo much needed spiritual medicine.

Season after season in my life, as you will notice, has been marked by receiving from God through His incredible family called the local church. May my story be a call to true community and the God who is the head of it all.

Without this dynamic duo, the forthcoming story would not exist. The fact is, Jesus does not throw in the towel when others do. He does not even throw in the towel when *we* do. His love is reckless, and His pursuit is constant. Nothing we go through will be wasted. With this book, I've attempted to squeeze all the juice out of my story that I can. I'm now handing you the glass for a drink.

You have permission to weave yourself into my narrative. If you relate to my missteps, know that the God who corrected my course will do the same for you. If you connect with my victories, you best believe that God will duplicate them in your midst as well. By all means, draw insight from the setbacks and glean inspiration from the comebacks. At the end of the day, my story is yours.

Read, relax, and receive.

CHAPTER ONE

STARTING EARLY

I t was a little past 5 a.m. and I was a little past 5 years old. The sun was not up yet, but I was. The living room was dimly lit, and there I sat, *praying*. I was getting heaven's attention from our small home in southern Arkansas. Was I a spiritual prodigy? Not in the slightest. Was I the son of folks who had mandatory prayer meetings at 5:30 a.m. every weekday morning? You better believe it.

My three siblings and I didn't usually leave our bedroom with praise, nor did we always enter the living room with thanksgiving. It was a slog to get up and pray at times. Yet the value of connecting with Jesus was put into us and eventually, the *discipline* of prayer taught me to *delight* in prayer.

Under any normal circumstances, after a week of early prayer meetings, I would be sleeping in on the weekends. The problem was, most Saturdays were spent in the woods hunting small game before the crack of dawn. When that was not happening, it was a common occurrence to spend the day with my dad passing out tracts in town to win souls. We were evangelical to the bone.

Ministry was as normal as breathing. It was baked into our home culture. When we kids were young, Dad would put on Disney and say, "I'll be back in an hour." Mickey Mouse babysat us while he would run over to the nursing home, pray for as many people as he could, and rush back home. Eventually when we got old enough, he would take us, too. The service outline was simple: he would preach and the kids would sing. It wasn't necessarily a *joyful* sound unto the Lord—but it was a sound no less. To accompany the singing, I played tuba in the school band so I would occasionally take my instrument into the nursing home and play "Amazing Grace." There was nothing amazing nor graceful about it. Nevertheless, the low-pitch blast had a way of waking up the congregants.

Those eventful Saturdays were then punctuated by a Sunday churchathon. If you grew up in a Christian home in the south, you know Sundays are an ordeal. Services were so long we got *benchlash*. That's the church pew version of *whiplash*. We, by no means, were allowed to just go through the motions either. Mom would instruct us in the ways of worship.

"Bring the sacrifice of praise. Lift your hands. Worship the Lord. It don't matter how you feel, push through. Enter in."

There were times we didn't get out of church until 3 in the afternoon—stomachs growling louder than the closing prayer.

Even family dinners were not short on Scripture. In order to come to the table to eat, you had to have a passage memorized. Once you recited it, you could dig in. I remember thinking I had found a shortcut on one occasion.

"Chris... your Scripture?"

"Jesus wept."

"You're gonna be weeping *with* Jesus if you come back with that again!"

That loophole did not impress my folks. Dad had not always been a man of faith. In fact, he gave his life to Jesus the same year I was born, in 1977. He and my mom attended Lakewood Church in Houston, which was pastored by John Osteen at the time. They cut their teeth on preachers like Fred Price, Charles Capps, Norvel Hayes, Kenneth Hagin, and other generals of that variety. Their impact cannot be measured. In fact, I could walk into my folks' house today, the same one I grew up in, and find all of those Word of Faith cassettes—and they are not collecting dust either. They're still being played and amen'd.

When my parents were saved and filled with the Holy Spirit in the late '70s, it changed everything. We were living in Texas at the time, but my parents knew they needed to get back to Arkansas, their birthplace, to give away what they had just received. Leaving behind good jobs and stable income, they left Texas when

I was in first grade. They knew where they needed to go: Camden.

Camden had been my father's birthplace. My mother, though, was born near the Louisiana border in Crossett. Both my parents were raised in the small town, everybody-knows-everybody's-business type of setting. Because of that, when Mom and Dad met at the University of Pine Bluff, one of the oldest institutions in Arkansas, there was no culture shock. They quickly knew they were right for each other. It was a standard mid-century, southern courtship. They were married shortly after with no fanfare. In fact, the ceremony took place inside of a living room in Camden.

With all of these deep ties to the area, my parents were excited to settle down and bring their new-found Holy Ghost power to Arkansas. We moved into my childhood home, a two-bedroom house, where I shared a room with my older brother Anthony, my little brother Stephen, and eventually our little sister Andrea. Dad took a job at a plant making $5 per hour and would preach any chance he could, to whoever would invite him.

Because he grew up in the Baptist church, it only made sense that he would preach in those same circles. The problem was, he was bringing a doctrine of the gifts of the Spirit to the pulpit, which was more than a little taboo for a Southern Baptist congregation. It went over like a lead balloon.

In fact, they had attended Damascus Baptist Church for years, and when the longtime pastor died, it only made sense that my dad would inherit the church and become senior pastor. They did not give it to him though, because he believed in the baptism of the Holy Spirit. That was dangerous to their doctrine.

This hurt my father, as you might imagine. He later linked up with a man named Jerry Ables and began to change their city with church plants and the proclamation of the full gospel. They still run together to this day and have brought genuine, societal change to that area. I so appreciate Jerry, not only for the friend he was to my dad, but he was like a spiritual father to me. With him also being the father of my best friend, Cricket, I spent many hours over at their house.

Dad was always a preacher. He favored R.W. Schambach, and had the preaching style to go with it. Mom has always been a teacher. The difference? A preacher *proclaims* whereas a teacher *explains*. Together, they balanced each other out in more ways than one.

From the time I could walk, throughout my childhood, I was really close with my mom. I was with her all the time, clinging to her the way some kids cling to a blanket. She offered a levity that was sometimes lacking with my dad. With Dad, he would get off work, put his things down, and pray for an hour in the living room. If you caught him before that prayer took place, you had to feel out where he was and tread carefully. If he had been through a rough day, you had better test the water. He was no teddy bear.

It could be a strict, no-nonsense environment. He wanted what was best for us, and his means to get us there was order and structure. We knew he loved us, though. He would come to tears when praying for us kids and his sacrificial love was felt. Later in life, I came to appreciate some of his serious, stoic nature and can see some of it in myself.

Yet I also see much of my mom's influence in me. She was more cheerful and carried conversations on with us kids. She would ask about our day, and often, she already knew about our day due to her being a teacher at the private school we attended. She taught algebra, English, and French, and eventually became the principal of the entire joint. Mom was quick to joke and laugh. She was and is affectionate, kind-hearted, and taught us the ways of Jesus in a way that she herself did not get from her own parents.

Not only were my parents good for their kids, but they were, and still are, good for their community. They were *always* helping people. As a pastor now, I can honestly say I first saw true pastoral care fleshed out long before I entered the ministry. I saw it at home as a child. It was rare that a week would pass without someone being at the house receiving prayer or counsel. It did not matter what was needed, Mom and Dad were faithfully available.

Beyond the outdoors, I took a liking to sports. Physically, I was a gifted kid and found a home on the offensive line. I was a shy child, more standoffish than my other siblings—but there was nothing shy about the way I hit people on the field. In full disclosure, I hit people *off* the field, too. In fact, the reason I was pulled out of public school and into private school was my fighting.

Unresolved internal issues and anger toward the world led me to throw hands anytime, anywhere. Having an older brother meant I learned the ins and outs of fighting early. I had dealt with some bullies and felt low on self-esteem, and I wasn't as close to my dad as I wanted to be. This cocktail mixture of feelings all manifested as resentment toward everything. Children are not meant to be angry all the time, but I was. Children are meant to be happy. I was not. In fact, I first tasted depression at the ripe old age of 6.

Depression was an emotional nuke, leveling all the good feelings a child should experience. It was heavy, grim, dark, with no way out. The attack on my life from such a young age could only mean that God was gearing up for something extraordinary—but I could not see that at the time.

My mind, body, and spirit were all under fire. Depression is reinforced by hopelessness. It's like being lost in the desert, without so much as a mirage to give you even a false sense of hope.

Fight after fight, I became colder and colder. With each swing, I was growing emotional callouses. My conscience was seared, numb, and I had very little sensitivity to the Lord or to the feelings of others. At one point, my parents got a call from one of my coaches.

"Mr. and Mrs. McRae, there's something off with Chris."

"Go on."

"He is angry. Really angry. When he hits somebody on the field, it's not just a tackle. He hits to hurt. There's rage behind that helmet. Is everything okay at home?"

Everything was okay in the home, but far from okay in my heart.

I was the go-to guy when someone got into a fight. I had a buddy named Cricket, who would occasionally loop me into scraps that he had going. He would arrive at the house with the offer.

"Chris, I need you to help me fight this group of guys."

"I'm in."

I didn't need to know how many or how big. It was on. I would get so lost in rage I would almost snap out of it and find myself with bloody hands in the middle of the fight. In my heart of hearts, down deep, I actually didn't want to hurt people. It did not do anything for me. There was no long-term gratification in being the tough guy. I was hurting personally—**and hurting people hurt people.**

I was in for a head-on collision with the God who could handle my punches and diffuse my rage. He was not put off by my short fuse. He didn't shy away from the mean kid from Camden. Perhaps I had read the verse, "The Lord is *slow* to anger, abounding in stead-fast love" (see Numbers 14:18). I just hadn't yet *become* the verse. That was to change, as God was soon to re-place my resentment and cause an internal one-eighty.

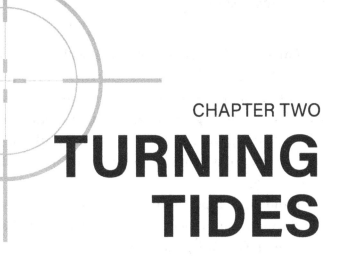

CHAPTER TWO

TURNING TIDES

"What do you want to be when you grow up?" I had no answer to that question.

Most kids have dreams and aspirations of being somebody or doing something big for the world. When I think about my childhood, I really did not have these kinds of ambitions. I coasted. With a solid C average in the classroom, the Ivy Leagues weren't exactly eyeballing me. I didn't daydream about being an astronaut. I didn't aspire to be a fireman. I had no set plan or path. God certainly did. I just wasn't privy to it at the time.

I was in church every week. I had heard the gospel countless times. I had Scripture memorized. I was on a first name basis with Jesus. However, I had not fully *given myself* to Him. Shaking hands with someone is different than surrendering to them. I had only shaken hands with the Lord, so to speak.

I may have had a meet-and-greet with Jesus in children's church, but He was not officially on the throne of my life. I sort of knew Him through my parents. But God does not have grandkids. He wants children of His own. I had piggybacked off my parent's faith for long enough and a day came when He asked for my full and complete *yes*.

It did not happen at the altar. God did not beckon me during a camp meeting. No, it happened after an episode of *The Cosby Show*. What does a person need in order to get saved? Well, you don't need a spiritual setting. You need a *surrendered soul*—which I happened to have that night.

The memory is as clear to me as anything. The closing credits of *The Cosby Show* started rolling, saxophone and all. NBC's nightly news followed and my mind began turning. The Cold War was being hyped. Fear was coming through the airwaves. Questions and uncertainty seemed to be everywhere—not unlike today. My eight-year-old self was feeling overwhelmed. I could not place my finger on what I was feeling precisely, but something was shifting in me.

I made my way into the bedroom, knelt down, and began to think. I was troubled. I was concerned. I was convicted. I looked inside myself and I did not like what I could see. Somehow I knew there was a gap between God and me, and it was a gap that I could not live with any longer. My mom came in and knelt next to me, leaning against that ugly brown bedspread. That conversation is still vivid to me almost 40 years later.

"What's wrong?"

I spoke intentionally and sincerely. "I don't really know Jesus like I should. I think I need to receive Him as Lord of my life."

Her heart must have swelled with joy. Their prayers, which were constant, were coming to fruition. It was unprovoked. Nobody had pressured me to *pray a prayer*. I was not guilted into salvation. I was not thrown into a baptismal tank against my will. It was not a standard raise your hand, repeat a phrase, and check a box at VBS sort of protocol. It was a true, organic, God-inspired conversion.

"Let's pray," she said.

I carefully repeated her words. The prayer covered all the bases. "Dear Lord Jesus, I believe You are the Son of God. You died for my sins, rose from the grave, and are coming again. Today I receive You as the Lord of my life. Forgive my sins and cleanse me. Help me to live for You. In Jesus' name, amen."

Most salvations are preceded by a sermon. Mine was preceded by a sitcom. The news that came after the show was my altar call. Thus, a theme was birthed in my life, that some of the richest miracles and encounters with God that I would have would take place in some of the most un-spiritual settings.

Nevertheless, it was a demarcation in time for me. I was actually, officially *born again*. Pretty soon, my childhood hero was not just Superman. Pastor John Osteen was added to that short list. Then again, they could have been the same person as far as I was concerned—I never saw both men in a room at the same time.

Getting saved added a new depth to my church

life. I had always enjoyed Willie George when he led children's ministry programs, way before he planted *Church on the Move*, but church took on a new meaning for me after my salvation. I even thought it might be interesting to work with kids in church one day. That thought left my mind as soon as it came, but it was prophetic, no less.

I loved and embraced the different church events that were happening in those days. I was stunned by the John Jacobs power team that came through. These men were big and they were strong, yet had a tenderness toward God that was genuine. My older brother Anthony and I made a pact that one day we would be part of a power team like that, tearing phone books and punching through cinder blocks. There was a lot that I admired about Anthony. He was always so good with people. Charismatic and easy going—more potential than you could imagine. I was the opposite. Even after my salvation, I was backwards. In social settings, I hid behind my mom and cowered from conversation. No one would have guessed that I would eventually become the guy with the microphone.

As I grew up, school didn't get easier, but sports did. I was big and could move people on the football field. When I wasn't moving opposing players, I was moving logs in the family business. My grandfather had started a logging company, outfitted with a pulpwood truck. He eventually handed the company to my dad who named it *Tree of Life, LLC.*

"Dad, we're *killing* trees. Why is the company called *Tree of LIFE?*"

No explanation was given. No explanation was needed. It was biblical and that was good enough.

Dad expected you to work hard. Often, before daylight, we would be cutting trees, hauling logs, and drenched in sweat. I recall asking him, "Dad, what time is it?"

"You taking medicine or something? Why do you need to know the time?"

Neither of my folks were impressed by excuses. If you had a valid excuse, like you got hit by a truck, for example, they would accept it. Otherwise, it was no-nonsense in the logging woods. Of course, this ran against the grain of my young mind, but slowly and surely, work ethic was being wired into me.

I was not born with a golden spoon in my mouth. Firstly, because my folks did not have one to give me. And secondly, even if they had one, they wouldn't have given it to me, because they were interested in raising a well-adjusted adult—not a coddled kid. As irritating as a hard-nosed upbringing can be, it's still paying me dividends decades later. At times, I wanted a blanket but was given sandpaper, so to speak. The rough edges of my character were being smoothed out.

The one thing you have in common with your parents, and your parents have in common with theirs, and so on, is that you have things you appreciate about your upbringing and things you would change about your upbringing if you could. Every generation has looked back and reflected on the pros and cons of their childhood. I am no different.

I did not get long speeches of affirmation and praise from my dad. He expressed joy and approval in subtler ways. We'd be driving out of the woods with a truckload of logs and he would deliver a solid slap to my thigh. Without saying anything with it, I knew he was pleased. It made a difference.

By the time I reached middle school age, I had been saved for a few years, but still had mounting anger. I had remained pretty cold and distant.

My parents were actually on the verge of taking me to see a psychiatrist. They were out of ideas. By this time, as a family, we were reading seven chapters of the Bible per day. Our parents required it before we went out to play with friends. So, the Word was in me, but something was still missing. I needed the duo of the Word and the Spirit.

Fed up with the unresolved pain and anger, I went to my room and sat in my blue chair, praying.

"God... I don't want to be this way. I don't want to be angry anymore."

I cannot accurately explain exactly what happened when I came to the Lord that day, but I can tell you everything changed. Holy Spirit came into that room and altered my heart. Joy replaced despair. Peace replaced restlessness. A heart of stone was replaced with a heart of flesh.

There was no worship music. There was no hyped atmosphere. Just Jesus. Much like my salvation years earlier, this encounter was not an external spectacle. But inside of me, a renovation had begun.

After leaving the room, I had a new outlook on life. It was as though the lens of my heart had been cleaned. I began making jokes with my family, teasing them and laughing. At first, I'm sure it caught them off guard. *Who was this new, kind Chris?*

I was no longer known by my scowl but by my smile. It became easy to bring levity into any situation—too much levity at times. But beyond those things, something greater happened—a love for people came into my heart. I started to care in very real and new ways about people's well-being. You could call it early pastoral instincts or simply a God-inspired selflessness, but regardless, things were different now. The world was more than me and my scruples.

Today, many folks know me as a pastor who jokes and laughs but fewer people know that it all started from a blue chair in my bedroom in Arkansas. In seed form, this is also where I received a gift to communicate. That gift might have been small, but I had the opportunity to fan the flame. My first invite to preach was at a network church event. It was a youth crusade. I did not ask for the gig, but I said yes when the invite came from a lady named Miss Cassandra.

When the night came, the area youth groups were gathered together. We had about 40 young people in the room. That was 40 more people than I had ever preached to. My dad also came to hear the message. Nervous, I was introduced and set my Bible on the pulpit as the introductory applause faded. Enunciating into the microphone as best I could, I powered through my passages and principles.

How did my sermon go overall? Horribly.

Apparently, the first time you grab the microphone and speak, you don't have the fluidity of John Osteen nor the stage presence of Fred Price. I probably still have the cassette tape, which I haven't revisited.

The sermon was Scripture heavy—which was good. But I lacked humor, unique illustrations, and smooth transitions. It was clunky and anointed with the spirit of awkward. I tried my best to lay a foundation and offer some encouragement. The message was probably received better than I realized at the time. After all, who was expecting much from a 12-year-old first-time preacher?

I felt a boost of consolation afterward when I overheard my dad talking to someone about the message. "That was a powerful word." While he was not directing those words to me, he did not need to. I felt them. I think he knew there was something more there—a potential to be a bona fide preacher.

Something else happened in the pulpit that night that was almost addictive—I felt and sensed the presence of God. The anointing was tangible, like it is today when I take the platform. It was as if God was smiling at me. Somehow I felt and sensed that I was smack dab in the middle of the will of God.

In the movie *Chariots of Fire*, Eric Liddell was running in the Olympics when he was being pressured to leave his track career to take to the mission field. In response, he famously said, "God made me fast. And when I run, I feel His pleasure."

I was feeling God's pleasure when I poured my heart out that night. I still feel it when I speak. It's not that God bases His approval of me on what I do or don't do for Him. It's that when I begin to share His Word, I get an overwhelming sense that I am doing the very thing I was put on the planet to do.

The message was not polished and perfect that night in 1989. My inflection did not captivate the crowd. My Scriptures did not wow my peers. But none of those things were necessary. What was necessary was for me to know that God was in it, and that God was pleased. Fine-tuning would come later.

CHAPTER THREE

COMING OF AGE

Some say, "I'm in church every time the doors are open." Growing up, not only was I there every time the doors were open, but I was the one who actually opened the doors.

More than once I complained, "Dad, I can't go. I'm sick."

"Well, church is the place to get healed. Come on, you're going."

I groaned. I wasn't trying to forsake the assembly altogether, like Hebrews warned about, I was just trying to fight a cold from my bed instead of a church pew.

By the time I hit 16 and could drive, most of my miles were spent going to and from church. Nothing was off limits—singing in youth choir, cleaning, event set up, ushering, you name it. Cecilia Chan said, "Do the *important*, not the *impressive*." The importance of every level of service was carved into my brain early.

With some speaking gigs under my belt, I was now being asked to open services, take up offerings, and even preach at our home church on occasion. It didn't take me long to get comfortable sharing in front of the crowds. I savored it. I truly wanted people to *see* what I was *saying*. That's not a figure of speech. My heart was, and still is, for the congregation to be able to *visualize* what I *verbalize*. I began sharing stories, illustrations, and adding my flair to the messages. It felt like I was coming into my own.

On the family front, our home life was solid in those days. My dad had started working at the mill. It was a good job with respectable money. Mom had a nice gig in those days, too, as the postmaster. Things were getting better. I was close with my siblings, too—mostly because we had no choice. We shared a room.

When you're immersed in the church world like we were, you are basically in the *people business*. It was good training because several of us kids wound up working with people in one way or another. I mentioned Anthony's natural way with people earlier in the book. My younger brother, Stephen, was similar, always charismatic and easy to talk to. He is now pastoring in Florida at Salty Church—baptizing people in the Atlantic and having church cookouts on the beach. Truly suffering for Christ. I'm the closest with him of all my siblings. Then again, all of us kids are closest with Stephen. He's the glue. Fun, wise, and full of Jesus, I try to talk to him once a week still.

My sister Andrea always had a nurturing spirit

growing up. While she didn't wind up in church ministry, she became a nurse who trains other nurses in San Diego, caring for patients, which is a ministry of its own. No doubt, those formative days in Camden made us who we are, for better or worse.

Beyond my parents, I had other mentors who shaped me. People like Stanley Clemmons, Bret Thomas, Steven Nine, Steven Willis, and Stacy Barron were instrumental. God used them to correct, direct, encourage, and enlighten me. Taking a walk down memory lane through my teenage years is actually a pleasant one because of men like them.

"Chris, you're destined for greatness. We believe in you."

These words of affirmation from them, as simple as they were, helped to *make me*. I loved them for it. They saw the gold in me and worked to mine it out. A good leader knows how to apply the perfect amount of pressure to coal in order to produce that diamond. They knew when to challenge me and when to encourage me, when to be tough and when to be tender. While many teens try to avoid their youth leaders outside of church, I *wanted* to be around mine.

I would help them any chance I could with moving things, building stuff, and getting my hands dirty. Some thought I was crazy for the amount of free help I gave them. In fact, if I sent them an invoice for my time spent helping them, I could probably retire right now. The truth is, *I was the one benefitting*. I was the one drawing from them. Not the other way around.

My dad had taught me work ethic and a "leave it better than you found it" mentality. But they helped to funnel that work ethic and mentality into all areas of ministry and life. On more than one occasion, they kept me out of trouble, too.

For example, I would get a call from a girl of interest inviting me to come over. To my dismay, the Lord, knowing nothing good would come of it, would have one of my mentors interfere. As soon as I was headed out the door, I'd get a call from Stanley.

"What are you doing?"

"Uh, nothing."

"Good. I need you to come on a hospital visit with me."

God used them to run interference between me and red flags. With Camden being a small town, everybody knew everybody's business. If you got in trouble, your parents knew about it before you got home, but when you add the fact that I had mentors who heard from God, I genuinely could not get away with anything.

I never had a wild spree as a teen, which I'm grateful for now. In fact, our potential to rebel was stymied by the fact that we couldn't even go out with friends on Saturday nights growing up.

Mom made it clear, "We need to have our minds and spirits settled and ready for church." Without fail, we were home, preparing ourselves for the Word that would follow in the morning. It was a process of ironing our clothes, getting our outfits approved, and resting up.

"There's still a wrinkle in that pant leg. Do it again," is a phrase I heard on the regular. While we might not be as militaristic and regimented now that I've got my own family, we do keep Saturday nights low key and preparatory for Sunday mornings in the house of God.

———

By my sophomore year, I was invited to spend the summer traveling with an evangelist named Leonard Ford. By that time, Leonard had been in the full time ministry for a decade, pioneering a prophetic and evangelistic ministry in the region. I was excited at the prospect. I was already serving in church all the time. I figured I might as well be serving in a different church every week for a summer.

We journeyed throughout Arkansas and Louisiana. I would help set up the tent, drive stakes, and carry chairs. My help extended beyond mere grunt work. Before our meetings, Leonard had me lead the pre-service prayer, as well as open for him each night. I was cutting my teeth in a new way, learning to preach and pray from a veteran.

God was cultivating a familiarity and a love for the ministry in me. To the surprise of many, some of the most influential figures in Scripture were teenagers when they began in the ministry. Jeremiah was first called as a teen, for example. In fact, he felt his youth had disqualified him. God had other ideas. Eventually that same bashful teen who said, "I cannot speak," eventually declared, "His word was in my heart like a burning fire shut up in my bones; I was weary of holding it back, and I could not" (Jeremiah 20:9).

Timothy was described as a "youth" by Paul, and was pastoring the church of Ephesus, one of the most influential churches in the first century. Many scholars agree that the disciples whom Jesus gathered were between 13 and 15 when He first called them for their three-year journey together. In a sense, Jesus was the original youth pastor.

Point is, God likes to stir up young people. We know statistically that around 94% of people who make a decision for Christ do so before the age of 18[1]. This is no joke. God likes to capture the youth, and He was certainly capturing me.

Around that time, we went to a service in Arkansas that was being led by a traveling minister named Robert Morris from Texas. He was powerful, dynamic, and flowed in the gifts of the Spirit. Everywhere he went, he had a knack for calling people out, reading their mail, and starting fires in all the right ways. This was seven years before he would start Gateway and eventually be launched into megachurch stardom.

Being a friend of the family, Robert was comfortable enough to give me a nickname: *tree trunk*, which he still lovingly refers to me with to this day. It was fitting for my stature. During that service, a watershed moment occurred when he took the stage.

"Tree trunk, stand up."

I did as I was told. Looking at me, he began to prophesy.

"You are going to be in ministry. I see you preaching, I see kids around you. There is *always* going to be a place in the church world for you. God bless you as you start your journey in ministry."

I sat down, unimpressed.

After the service, my friends and I went out to grab a bite to eat. "He missed that word big time. I'm going to play football."

Sure, I enjoyed speaking when I could, but ministry as a long-term career? Forget it. It's one thing to serve on a Sunday, but operating in a church office during the week was not on my wish list. I was bound to be a layman. Not ordained clergy. I was not appalled by the notion, like Moses arguing with God at the burning bush, but I simply was not drawn to it whatsoever.

Many years later, in May of 2017, Pastor Robert would be handing me a ministry diploma from King's University. Knowing I had spent my entire adult life in ministry, he quipped, "Hey, tree trunk... how 'bout that word I gave you back in the day?"

He had nailed it.

CHAPTER FOUR

DESTINATION DALLAS

"Don't step on the twigs. Keep your feet light. Walk where I walk." Dad was not short on instruction when I hunted with him. He taught me to love the outdoors. Maybe it was an outlet for frustration. Maybe it was an inlet for peace. Perhaps both. With the Ouachita River in our backyard, I could walk outside and be in the woods or in the water within 30 seconds. Some of my fondest and earliest memories are of walking into the woods with Dad, him carrying a 16-gauge bolt action shotgun and me with a single-shot .22 rifle. Squirrels and rabbits beware.

My job was simple: keep track of where his feet landed and step in that same spot. If I didn't do that, I'd snap a branch or ruffle leaves and compromise our hunt—and he would let me know about it. Following his footsteps was more prophetic than I realized at the time.

We are not called to blaze our own trail. God does not expect *us* to lead the way. He does that. Our role is to humbly step where He steps. To say what He says and to do what He does is the epitome of the Christian life. In the same way that I mimicked my dad's footsteps in the woods, it was time to mimic the footsteps of Jesus in my plans after my senior year.

As high school progressed, I had decisions to make. No matter what happened after school, I knew I needed to leave the small town. When the mill eventually shut down, the town got even smaller to where it now sits at a population of about 13,000. Thank God I got out when I did.

For some time, I really wanted to join the army. As regimented and strict as my upbringing was, the army would feel like a play date. I was drawn to the idea of service and wearing the uniform for our nation. I had talked to recruiters at school and the plans started to seem real. However, when my mom begged me with tears in her eyes to not join, I reluctantly dropped the idea. Besides, it became clear that given my size and strength, I had a chance to go a long way with football.

I told my dad I would play football at Arkansas University. I was a force to be reckoned with on the field and knew I could get the attention of scouts. I was powerlifting competitively and was 4th in the nation in my division. I was big and strong, and had the John Wayne sort of grit to go with it. The athletically-charged plan was in place, and I even had a stamp of approval from my folks.

It was around that time that God used a classmate of mine named Don Goodwin III to disrupt all of my well-formulated blueprints.

"Chris, you've got to come to this *eternity weekend* with me in Dallas."

"What's it about?" I was skeptical but interested.

"It's a conference at Christ for the Nations. The Bible school."

His parents were alumni and had connections at the school. Don was really just going to see his girlfriend who lived in Dallas and wanted a buddy to tag along for the trip. He was chasing a girl, not an encounter with God. The only familiarity I had with the school was hearing a CFNI worship album from some youth leaders. Otherwise, I didn't know what to expect, but I agreed to go. Don and I got along well, and I figured it would be a good time—nothing more, nothing less. But bigger things were awaiting me on the other side of that 4-hour drive to Texas.

———

Not long into the conference, I was sitting in service and heard a voice. It wasn't the person sitting next to me. It wasn't the preacher. It wasn't my own internal dialogue. It was God—and He had news for me.

"You're going to be going to school here."

With one sentence from heaven, my NCAA dreams of grandeur were out the window. Funny enough, I was somehow fine with that. Truth be told, I had not squeezed any dream so tight that it couldn't get away. That worked in my favor when God tweaked my destination.

I came home and broke it to my dad. His response was blunt, per usual.

"They don't have football at Christ for the Nations. You crazy?"

"I know. But it's what I heard."

"And you are *completely* sure you heard God on this?"

"Positive."

He didn't lose his cool, nor did he get upset knowing he wouldn't watch his boy smashing helmets with Ole Miss in a year. He put it plain to me, "Count the cost, son."

He knew the potential career I was giving up. He saw me compete and knew I could compete at the college level. I did heed his wisdom, though. I counted the cost. I was aware that the idea would be considered silly to the world. Yet I couldn't run from what I knew God was saying. The will of God was worth the price.

When God speaks, it often starts in seed form— small, subtle, carrying only a little weight. Yet the *rhema* word seems to grow internally and solidify more and more over time. This was no different. My plans may not have been taking shape like I thought they would, but at the very least, I had full faith in the new direction.

After that conversation with dad, that was the end of it. There was no more discussion about athletics after high school. To my parent's credit, they *never* pushed me to be anybody or anything except what God wanted me to be. I didn't grow up with a thumb in the back of my neck, pressured to fit a mold.

Dad did circle back to me some weeks later to have another type of conversation. This time, it was about how I'd be spending my summer after graduation.

"I got you a job at the mill. You're going to work all summer long. Playtime is over."

I hadn't been coddled at any point growing up, so this type of conversation was easily received. When we looked at the tuition rates, he did not hand me his checkbook. He handed me a job application.

"You're gonna save up money and pay for your first semester of school."

I finally walked across the stage in May of '95. High School Graduation is not a conclusion but a *commencement,* which means "a beginning" or "a start." This *start* means different things to different people. For some, it means law school. For others, it means the army. For me, it meant stashing cash all summer because I was Dallas bound and proud of it.

I was a Pipe Insulator at the mill, working hard from 7 a.m. to 3:30 p.m. daily. Several friends, as well as my cousin Jabarre, worked there, which made for a good environment. We were all doing the same thing: raising money for school. It was hot, physical work. Logs would come in and I would oversee the steam pipes, making sure they were insulated and ready to go.

I made the most of that summer fishing, camping, and playing church softball outside of work. It came and went quickly. By the time August rolled around, reality was setting in. I was about to kiss my hometown goodbye, *for good*. I was not going to be a small-town boy any longer.

Some friends of my parents had a business in Dallas and offered to take me and help me get settled into the city. Another couple in the church heard about my new venture and gave me a 1983 Cutlass Supreme. The grace of God was covering me where the will of God was leading me.

It was a Friday in August 1995 when I left Camden. I gave my dad a simple side hug. It was a straightforward departure. Even though I would see him in Dallas a few days later, where he would help me get settled into my dorm, this goodbye felt different. It was heavier. His roof was not over my head any longer. I was glad to be going but still felt the usual whirlwind of emotion. Was I nervous? Sure. But I still had a decent helping of unearned confidence. I felt like an adult, like I was ready for the world. Many years later when my oldest child hit 18, I was finally able to grasp just how young that truly is.

Armed with the prayers of my parents and enough cash to last me a little while, I put the Cutlass in drive and left Camden. It was more than my hometown in the rearview mirror. It was my childhood, my upbringing, the stuff that built me. This was my Rubicon to cross.

I approached Dallas at night, city lights glowing and high-rise buildings coloring the sky. I was not in rural Arkansas anymore. Reality set it. *I can't believe I'll actually be living here!* I was a bit intimidated, but ready for the challenge. My host family took me to a Rangers game the very next day and I started to feel at home quicker than I thought I would.

When I got to the campus, my dad had come to help me find my dorm. He looked around the room. He was quiet. So was I. He sat down on the bed. Everything was taken care of, except the goodbye.

"Alright, son. Don't you be down here makin' a fool of me at this school."

Yes, sir.

That was about as much as was communicated as we said our farewells. He kept it brief and kept it together, at least until he got to his car. Many years later, I learned that he had shed tears on the drive home. Dallas was right for me, and he knew it, but that did not make leaving me any easier. Plus, he knew what I didn't know then, that 18 is way younger than you think it is. Nevertheless, I was out of the nest. Time to fly or die.

As I unpacked and settled into campus, it was getting real. I explored the landscape, learned as much as I could, and started meeting people quickly. Over the next several months and years, the reasons why God had me in this city would continue to pile up. For now, I was a newbie with a couple suitcases' worth of possessions, a solid heart, and a naive head.

CHAPTER FIVE

BIBLE SCHOOL

The last time I had lived in Texas, I was taking the 10¢ metro bus to my elementary school in Houston. Now, I was stepping foot onto a first-class campus to lean in and learn as much as I could. The place was nothing short of amazing. The excitement, the student body, the facilities, the faculty—it was a supreme operation. The place was teeming with anticipation.

At that time, there were 1,200 students, which was peak enrollment since Gordon Lindsey had founded it in 1970. Lindsey was a scribe who had spent years documenting healings for the likes of John Alexander Dowie. So when he founded the school, that tutelage definitely informed Lindsey's approach to the gospel, which meant healing, miracles, and the move of the Spirit were all baked into the culture and teaching at Christ for the Nations Institute. To me, that felt like home. All these years later, I'm still fairly close with Gordon Lindsey's grandson and maintain some involvement with the school as an alumnus.

Prior to attending, I had certainly experienced the Holy Ghost. From the Cosby show conversion to the blue chair baptism, I had my fair share of encounters with God. Yet things ramped up in Dallas. The school would have itinerant speakers in regularly, some who left an indelible mark on me.

On one occasion, I found myself on the floor of the auditorium, looking at the ceiling. I hadn't slipped. I hadn't lost a fight. No, I had been called out among a sea of students by an evangelist named James Malone. I was thoroughly slain in the Spirit. The mixture of uncontrollable laughter and crying that followed was probably a *Holy Ghost heart surgery* that went deeper than I was aware of at the time.

We worshiped every morning at 8 o'clock sharp on campus. This was rich, impactful, and imparted a hunger for the presence of God in me. This 8 o'clock meeting felt like sleeping in, compared to our living room rendezvous growing up.

As far as the regular classes went, I don't remember much about them. That's not because I was hungover or sleep deprived, like many folks' college experience. Instead, I was intoxicated by something else—a subtle sense of pride. We were taught Christianity 101. It was the basics, the fundamentals. On more than one occasion I thought, *I could be teaching this class.*

I saw it all as boring and stale, like a saltine cracker that you'd pull out of the back of the cupboard. In retrospect, I should have viewed it as the meat and potatoes of the Christian life. It may not have had the flair and the excitement of a fancy dessert, but the basic meat and potatoes of the gospel truly are the sustaining force of our lives. I sat in the back, slept a little, goofed off a lot, talked too much, and threw most of the teaching into a box labeled, "Stuff I already know."

If I could go back, look myself in the eyes, and slap myself with some wisdom, I would say, "Chris, you know less than you think you do. And the stuff you think you know, you don't know as well as you could."

Charles Spurgeon wrote, "A student will find that his mental constitution is more affected by one book thoroughly mastered than by twenty books he has merely skimmed." I was in the latter category. I knew the Bible front to back. I had covered a lot of territory in the Scriptures and sat through more sermons than I could count. I had gone wide; I just hadn't gone deep.

Because of all this, when I'm asked, "What did you get out of Bible school?" my answer is usually, "A wife."

After all, CFNI sounds a lot like *seein'-if-I* can find a spouse.

———

Vanessa Cooke was sitting on a bench on the school property when I noticed her. I was with friends, meandering and passing time. Unlike the lectures, I wanted to approach this mystery girl with some degree of seriousness. I introduced myself and we chatted for a while. It was a fairly tight-knit student body, so over the course of several weeks, we would be around each other often.

Her first impression of me was that I was *mean*. This wasn't because of bad behavior, but because I was quiet and standoffish at first. I was slow to open up, but once I did, I was a bona fide extravert.

She, on the other hand, was an *introvert*. I didn't want to end up with a female version of myself and she didn't want to end up with a male version of herself. So, as is often the case, opposites attracted.

The attraction wasn't instant though. She didn't know what to make of me in the beginning. I was a bit of a puzzle. Whether she knew it at the time or not, she would spend a lifetime trying to put that puzzle together.

Because I was a big guy with a big personality, my friend group was large, and I had a number of friends who were girls. In fact, I had a different girl cooking for me about every night of the week. Lasagna on Monday from this one. Chicken on Tuesday from that one. I had no complaints.

As I became more and more focused on Vanessa, she wasn't convinced I was interested in her. Reason being, she thought I was trying to make friends with her in order to get to her roommate. When she expressed that to her friends, they advised, "No... I think he is trying to get to *you*, Vanessa."

She went about testing the waters. She must have figured, if the quickest way to a man's heart was through his stomach, then the quickest way to his stomach is with a cheesecake. She lovingly made it and brought it to me. The crust, the filling, the topping—it all looked perfect.

I put it in my room to save it for later. When I came home later that night, I was horrified at what I saw. My roommate had the cheesecake in a headlock, and with a fork in one hand, was eating right out of the middle of it. I was heated and ripped into him. When Vanessa later asked for a review of her work, I had to confess what happened.

"How'd you like the cheesecake?"

"You aren't going to believe this. I was keeping it till later and my stupid roommate found it and ate it."

Somehow, she wasn't shocked.

"I knew that was going to happen. Here's another one."

She had a replacement prepared. That got my attention. Other girls might have cooked for me, but nobody had backups ready.

The days became weeks, weeks became months, and although I wasn't learning much in class, I was learning more and more about Vanessa. It was a blossoming friendship. I learned that she was from New Hampshire. I learned that she had wanted to be a missionary. I discovered that her spiritual parents introduced her to CFNI and that, like me, God had spoken to her to attend school there.

She had a Catholic background, but got saved in a Vineyard church years earlier. When her father passed away, early on in our friendship, it was a tragedy and truly hard on her. Not only was her dad gone, but she was set to grieve in a new city with no family or familiarity around. I called and checked on her every day. In fact, my concern for her during that season was one thing that helped tie us together.

Eventually we started going steady. My buddies would take a look at the Dodge Caravan she drove and quip, "She's ready for kids already, Chris. Better get ready." It was true that she knew from an early age that she would be a mom, and a good one. In fact, we worked with kids at the YMCA together while dating. I didn't know it at the time, but she was sizing up what kind of a dad I would be with not-so-subtle question-naires.

"If you had kids of your own and one of them bit the other, how would you respond?"

She had plenty of hypotheticals like this lined up for me. My answers must have been enough to pass her litmus test because we kept dating.

The relationship progressed until one day I was on a drive in my beat-up car from Carrollton to Dallas. I went before the Lord in prayer. I've found that your car can become a prayer closet if you want it to be. Vanessa and I had been dating for over two years and before I invested another second into the relationship, I needed an absolute *yes* from God.

"Lord, I need to hear You about this relationship. Am I supposed to marry Vanessa?"

I was as sincere as I had ever been. God answered my question with a question.

"Why not?"

It was as if God was extending an invitation for me to give Him my objections to marrying Vanessa. I didn't have any. In my spirit, I could sense Him asking, "Tell me, is there something you see that would forbid you from marrying her?"

I looked through Scriptures and didn't see anything keeping us from marrying at all. I felt His blessing, His seal of approval. Outside of entering a relationship with Jesus, I knew that entering a covenant marriage was the most consequential decision a person could make. I had too much to lose to screw that up.

"Chris, this is your choice... and I know it's a good one."

I had been working at Delta Airlines, saving up money, and was able to snag a ring for her at Zales. She picked it out. That said, when I proposed at Ruth's Chris Steak House in Dallas, she was not caught off guard.

With the box open and one knee on the ground, I popped the question. She had tears in her eyes and I had tears in mine, too. It was then that I heard that sought after three letter response.

Back home in Arkansas, things were not on cloud nine. My parents were not fond of the relationship. They grew up in the south during a time of rampant racism and had questions about how a black man and white woman would mesh long term. Their hesitations were not rooted in any sort of ill will on their part. Their concerns stemmed from their very real experiences in seeing cultures clash. This led to some heated discussions. They had their reasons, but I had mine. Most importantly, I felt my reasons were framed up by the will of God, which I did not take lightly.

In all seriousness, I was fine with unplugging from

my parents completely and marrying Vanessa without the slightest hint of their blessing. I was a man with a word from God. It's no surprise that this was hard on my new fiancé. She wanted their blessing. In fact, it became a *requirement* for her.

The day before we were set to get married, we had a Boeing 767 come in and I was going to work it, get married the next day, and fly to Honolulu for the honeymoon after that. Delta offered incredible flight benefits that we took advantage of.

I got a call from Vanessa during that shift.

"We have to call off this wedding. I cannot marry you without your parents agreeing to it."

My heart traveled to my stomach quickly.

"But we talked about this... we have people coming in... flights booked..."

I went to my supervisor and explained that I needed to run home to take care of something.

I found Vanessa on the porch, crying.

"Chris, I just can't do it without their blessing. You'll regret marrying me for the rest of your life if we go ahead with this and burn bridges with your family."

There were no negotiations about it. She was serious.

She continued, "Ring them and tell them we are willing to call off the wedding. We will come to Arkansas, meet, talk, and go from there."

With a heavy heart, I called off the wedding, the flights, lost money on cake, hotels, and more. Shortly after, we were Camden-bound. We didn't know what to expect. Our fears were eased the second we walked through the door. Vanessa and my folks hit it off. The conversations were fluid, understanding was built, and all was made well. Any issues or qualms were put to rest during that trip. We had won them over and received their blessing.

The wedding was rescheduled for 6 months later without the fanfare of the first one. You could count the number of attendees who were present with two hands. We were married on May 24th, 1998 in the prayer room at church.

To this day, 25 years later, my folks still apologize to Vanessa for doubting things in those early days. Of course, she has been over those hurts for decades and they have an amazing relationship.

Why is this worth sharing? Because often, people look at a couple in leadership or in the pastorate and think, *wow, they must have had the perfect dating relationship, the ideal engagement, zero in-law issues, a spotless wedding, and a trouble-free marriage.* In reality, a relationship may have God's green light, yet you may still feel some intense turbulence, to mix metaphors.

Early in our marriage, I continued loading airplanes and working the runway for Delta, a job I wound up having for eight years in total. I really liked that gig. It was the perfect setup for a student. The flight benefits meant Vanessa could go back to New Hampshire to see her mom whenever she needed to.

The schedule was also favorable. I would get out of school at noon, grab lunch, work a plane at 2 p.m., push it out to the runway, then have a couple hours to do nothing until the next flight would come in. The ample downtime meant I could study, read books, do homework, or do nothing at all. When we had taken care of the last plane of the night, I left at 10 p.m. and went home.

Home was a studio apartment on the property of the family that Vanessa nannied for. It was tight. Tight as in *small*, not fashionable. We cooked on hotplates and had minimal furniture. On the bright side, it was free. That made a big difference to us cash-crunched newlyweds.

Vanessa and I were learning to do life together. Like any first-year marriage, there were growing pains. I occasionally showed up to work with headaches, backaches, and wife-aches. We began to realize that those pesky opposite qualities that attracted us to each other could also repel us from each other if we didn't lean in with love.

She was a quiet white girl from New Hampshire. I was an extraverted black guy from Arkansas. She is a producer who makes money. I'm a people-person who spends money. She is much like my mom, and I am much like her dad. It was a big adjustment at every level.

We had to navigate the fact that we could no longer just walk out the door and leave to go wherever we wanted. Who would have thought that we actually had to inform our spouse of our plans? The fights seemed to happen more and more between us. In the mix of that season, I came across a teaching on how *the blessing* can change everything in marriage.

On a casual trip to Dallas during year one, my dad brought it up.

"You know, I never gave you guys my blessing."

"Sure you did," I reassured him.

"No, I gave the relationship my blessing, but I never *prayed* a blessing over your marriage."

There was a difference.

Vanessa and I joined hands. My dad laid hands on us and decreed a legitimate blessing over our marriage that changed everything, literally. The fights stopped. Love flowed freely. Disagreements and conflict continued, and they *will* continue as long as we are on the planet together. However, they weren't nearly as heated or life-and-death feeling. The intensity and the frequency totally changed.

Looking back, I wonder how our story might have been different, had we rushed ahead with the marriage and cut ties with my folks. How rocky would things have gotten, had my dad not been there to speak a blessing over us? He was, and is, not only a father but a *spiritual father*—something that not everyone can say about their dads.

In those days, I gained yet another spiritual father. He would come to have as much impact as my biological father and I would come to love him in the same way. Yet before that would come to pass, a scuffle in a church parking lot stood in the way.

CHAPTER SIX

JOURNEY TO SOJOURN

You can't swing a dead cat in Dallas without hitting a church. I had a banquet of world class ministries I could be a part of right in my backyard. The Metroplex region is chock full of powerhouse organizations that are doing incredible things for Jesus. While in school, I had my sights set on Potter's House. In fact, I really wanted to be a bodyguard for TD Jakes. I had worked some security jobs in the past and figured with my ministry chops, I would fit right in. Plus, I had the muscle to squash anyone with the nerve to threaten the man of God.

As part of my first-year requirements at CFNI, we had to take part in an evangelistic outreach ministry. I chose to witness at the Cedar Springs strip in Dallas. I grew up passing out tracts, so evangelizing in college was as natural as breathing. On top of the evangelism, though, I had to get an internship in a ministry because I was living off campus. That was something I had *not* done prior.

A man from my hometown in Arkansas had moved to Carrollton, Texas, to work for a gentleman named Steve Dulin, someone I had previously worked for in the construction field. With ties to both my hometown in Arkansas and my new home in Texas, Steve and I had some rapport. On top of running a construction company, he was an elder at a place called Sojourn Church in Carrollton. At one point he casually mentioned, "Why don't you come help us with the kids while we have lifegroup?"

We got credit hours for it and it would check my internship box, so I figured *why not?*

The door was opened and I closed out the millennium with a Sojourn internship where I would be involved in all things related to children's ministry alongside Vanessa. Later on, that became involvement in janitorial work, too. I wanted the *glory,* but wound up with the *grind.* It taught me a lot. If I am too good for the *lowest* job in the church, then I'm too proud for *any* job in the church. A servant does not choose his or her tasks like they are items on a menu.

"Yeah, I'll take a large ministry platform with a side of fame... and hold the persecution, please."

No, a servant just serves, regardless of income and outcome.

If the dirty, sweaty feet of the disciples were not below Jesus, then the toilet of a church was not below me. Besides, the outsized ego of a Bible school student ought to be bruised every now and then. The early days of ministry pulled no punches.

Initially, my time at Sojourn was purely work-related. We had church during the week at CFNI, so our time in the church in Carrollton was really just business. It's not that we did not enjoy it, it's just that it was not yet our home church where we would be anchored. When our internship had closed out, I wanted to see about that Potter's House role. Vanessa had other ideas.

During that season, God had spoken to us about attending Sojourn as our home church, but frankly, I wanted to explore other places. Nevertheless, she felt obliged to visit Sojourn. To be honest, I had a bad attitude about the situation from the start. When we showed up to the parking lot, I had shorts on. This may not seem like a crisis to you, the reader, but it was to me at the time. With my upbringing, you simply did not wear shorts to church. Ever. Plus, I needed an excuse to not go in. My ultimate destiny was Potter's House, after all.

We sat in the parking lot and I told Vanessa, "Why don't you just go in? I'm in shorts, I can't go in like this."

"Fine. You stay out here. I'm going in."

She has always had a mind of her own and I love that about her. She says what she means and means what she says. I could go haywire out of the blue and she would still be serving God regardless of my own mess. Independent of the opinions of man and fully dependent on Jesus is her sweet spot. In her mind, I should have put on something other than shorts before leaving the house. She was right. She had heard from

God about this church and I did, too. Maybe I figured if I delayed my obedience, God would change His mind.

Nevertheless, Vanessa went in and I sat there passing the time. As I did, an entourage exited the church. I gazed in my rearview mirror as the group of men seemed to be walking in my general direction. *Surely they're not coming out to talk to me,* I thought.

Sure enough, the holy mob got closer. An elder walked up to my driver's side window and gave it a couple taps.

"What are you doing out here?"

"I'm just waiting until service is over."

"You either come inside for church or leave the premises *right now.*"

I felt heat, and it wasn't the presence of God. I was so mad. I threw the car in reverse and pulled out of the parking lot as fast as I could. Had that elder been in the way, I might have hit him, leaving the church with a job opening on the welcome team.

I passed time around Carrollton rehearsing the incident and fuming until service was out. I rolled back over and picked up Vanessa. She noted that I wasn't in the spot I dropped her off.

"Where were you!?"

I told her what happened with great detail and steam. I then added, "And we are *never* coming back to this church again. We're going to Potter's House next week."

She was not moved by my impassioned speech in the slightest. In fact, she thought it was hilarious that I had been kicked off campus.

"No, Chris. We are coming back. God told us to be here, not at Potter's House or anywhere else for that matter. There's *something* here for us."

That "something" that she was sensing was a *church family*. A place to call home. A place to do life. A place to serve. A place to dedicate our future kids. A place to carry out the calling on my life that God had been ordering and planning from before I was in the womb.

Of course, before discovering all of this, I had a parking lot greeter to forgive. Ironically, that very elder who kicked me off the premise later helped vote me in to be on staff at Sojourn. All parties involved now laugh about the incident in retrospect.

With motivation from Vanessa, the next week I came back to Sojourn Church, with pants and all. Worship was good. The atmosphere was good. The people were engaged. The boxes were all checked. The church also seemed to have a rich history. It had been influenced heavily by the likes of John Wimber and the Vineyard movement.

The pastor valued the faith movement and adopted some principles, but wasn't a name-it-and-claim-it, blab-it-and-grab-it type of preacher. Sojourn had a heart for revival and dipped into streams like Toronto and Pensacola. Yet at the same time, they weren't trying to shoehorn a revival by burning out the church with services 7 nights a week.

Baptists would say the church was too wild and some in the charismatic movement might say the church was too tame and reserved. I noticed they sent and supported missionaries without sacrificing the local body. At the same time, they did not fixate so much on the local gathering that they forgot global missions.

The best word to describe what I was seeing was the word *balance*. The culture of Sojourn was stitched together with the tapestry of many movements and streams. At the end of the day, I saw a gathering and I saw leaders who wanted one thing: to know Jesus and to make Him known.

I had no complaints. I wasn't hooked, though, until the senior pastor, Terry Moore, took the pulpit. I didn't know anything about him at the time. He seemed like a good Texan who resembled John Wayne and had a gift to speak. Otherwise, I had no preconceived notions.

Not long into his message, I was gripped. He preached on the love of the Father—a message I had heard throughout my entire life. Yet at the same time, it was as if I was hearing it for the first time. It was an old, ancient message, yet Terry's take brought a fresh novelty to it in my heart.

"It's one thing to know the love of God mentally. It's another to have an actual *revelation* of the love of God in your heart. That cannot be stolen from you."

The love of the Father made the 18-inch leap from my head to my heart that day. I was compelled to come back. Week after week, he would surgically unpack topics like identity, freedom, and grace in ways I had never experienced. There was an ease to his approach. He didn't shout and stomp around the pulpit like I had experienced growing up. I do enjoy exhortation and fiery preaching, but he had an effortlessness in his teaching that I was gripped by.

Like an onion, he peeled back layers of the Bible. He examined issues from all sides and used the Word of God like a flashlight, to shed light on areas of our lives. Vanessa and I loved it. He would take us into deep water, but never without an oxygen mask. Both veterans and novices alike could pick up what he was putting down. Different guest speakers would come in and I would have my mind blown all over again.

I thought I was an expert on certain topics. Yet these folks would share and I realized I was not as seasoned as I thought I was. Their approach to teaching was captivating. I wanted to be a part of it. I figured I could take the content they were sharing, put my spin on it, and re-preach it. In fact, many of the sermons I preach today are messages that Terry preached in the '90s that I have workshopped, added illustrations to, and re-presented.

Pretty quickly I noticed so many similarities between Terry and my own father. They were both born on the same day of the same year. They were both *men's men* who liked to hunt. They were both long-term pastors, committed to the local flock. They each had Baptist backgrounds but ended up in the Spirit-filled movement. They even had the same football jersey number in high school. The only difference between the two was melanin levels.

It was easy to adopt Pastor Terry as a mentor and eventually a spiritual dad. I watched how he spent time with the Lord, how he loved his wife, and how he treated others. The freedom in the Spirit that he walked in was palatable. I wanted it for myself. Good leaders have contagious character like that. They don't just set an example, but cause an appetite in us to follow that example.

Pastor Terry took the time to invest, mentor, and get to know me. I simply made myself available. As much as I appreciated the different lecturers at Bible school, no one on campus was pouring into me like my pastor off campus.

"What's on your heart? What are you dreaming about? What has God called you to do?"

He was asking me questions that, frankly, I hadn't been asked before by my leaders. He had a genuine curiosity toward me. Sometimes I had answers and other times I didn't. Regardless, he helped me sift through where I was and where I should be. Often, under the guise of fishing or hunting, he would speak into me and truly pastor me. He cared for me like he cared for his own son.

In the same way my own dad taught me to walk and navigate life until it was time for me to leave home, Terry taught me how to walk and navigate new territory of faith and ministry. I learned how to love Jesus under my dad's ministry. I learned how to love people *like* Jesus under Terry's. Before I knew it, my ambition to be a Potter's House bouncer was gone.

CHAPTER SEVEN

OFFSPRING AND OPPORTUNITIES

I asked God for a microphone, but He gave me a toilet brush instead. So often we want a platform without pain. We want promotion without process. On more than one occasion, I found myself waist deep in "process." I was ready to win the world for Jesus, but Jesus was more interested in me taking out the trash than leading crusades. The Bible says, "Don't despise small beginnings" (Zechariah 4:10). If you despise small beginnings, you'll never get to the big endings.

At that time this felt cruel, because I had friends who worked for ministers like Tommy Tenney and other big shots. One day I got a call that, frankly, I resented.

"Chris, guess where I am?"

It was a Bible school buddy who was working for Jesse Duplantis.

"Where?"

"I'm on a jet! We are interviewing your pastor tonight on TBN. We are heading to the studio now."

The contrast was stark. He was traveling with world-renowned ministries and I was on the other end of the call, phone pinned between my shoulder and ear, pushing a janitor cart with big yellow gloves on my hands. I probably gave a half-hearted *congratulations*. I hung up and prayed.

"God, what am I doing here? My friends are traveling with huge ministers and I'm here cleaning bathrooms."

Like my parents growing up, He was not moved by my bellyaching. He was *building* me in order to *bless* me. Serving was my first stage and one I will never regret. Who was I to preach to people publicly who I was not willing to serve privately?

My attitude occasionally turned sour, and it seems like every time it did, Pastor Terry would walk into the room. I would turn off the vacuum or put down the Windex and he would encourage me.

I recall him once saying, "Chris, what you are doing is one of the most important jobs in the church."

There's no way. Your job is the most important, I thought.

He then added, "You're the first one in and the last one out. You set the tone. You can determine the temperature of the atmosphere. Pray over the people who will sit in these chairs. Visualize their faces and bless them before they even show up."

From then on, I made it a point to be the thermostat, so to speak, and to *pray in an atmosphere* wherein people could experience God. Instead of the gig being about me, I made it about the church. Over time, I developed a heart for the house. I would pray fervently, and before I knew it, I had vacuumed to the other side of the sanctuary. I would go back and sweep it again just so I could pray more.

During service times, Vanessa and I were loving the children's ministry. I had sat in enough children's church services growing up that I knew what would work and what would not. We mixed messages, songs, and games to provide a haven that the kids could rely on every week.

Looking back, I was learning more from Pastor Terry and hands-on internship than I did at CFNI. It's one thing to describe a motor and to discuss a wrench. It's another thing to pick up that tool and start turning bolts under the hood of a car. I was getting a real-world degree that trumped my time in the classroom.

My ministry's future was coming together before my eyes. I didn't see a reason to stick it out and finish my degree at CFNI. After two years there, I dropped out. Vanessa stayed and got her degree, and since we are *one* according to the Scriptures, I suppose that degree counts for me, too. Dropping out was not a matter of slacking, but a simple matter of logistics. I was running and gunning full force at Sojourn.

———

In the year 2000, two things happened. One, I became the junior high youth pastor at Sojourn Church. It was my first pastoral position and certainly not my last. Secondly, and most importantly, I became a dad.

Vanessa and I thought we could not have kids early on. We had tried for awhile to no avail, so when she showed me two lines on the test, I was stunned. It was overwhelming, exciting, and surreal. I remember feeling young and inexperienced also.

How could I be a dad, let alone a good one? Do I have what it takes? All the questions came in a wave.

In my head, I knew I was going to be a father. Yet before the baby comes you can't quite fathom what it's going to be like. I could read a book on parenting or attend a birthing class, but there's no substitute for having a dependent, adorable, diapered little piece of yourself in your arms.

We had been married just over a year and were thrilled to prepare for our little one. Vanessa went into nesting mode, and I continued working hard. The nine-month sprint to the delivery room was a time to grow up even more.

When I moved to Dallas, I became responsible for me. When I got married, I became responsible for her. In nine short months, I was going to be responsible for a child. It changes you and brings a sobriety to life. You begin to see things, not just differently, but *rightly*. Your value system gets a much-needed calibration.

As we got through the holiday season of 1999, Vanessa entered the third trimester. By the time spring approached, she and I were ready to see and hold this small miracle. It was Thursday, March 30, 2000 when Ainsley McRae was born. I was feeling the normal combo pack of new dad emotions. Joy, excitement, happiness, anxiousness, curiosity, affection; all the feelings were real and intense. The weight of responsibility is no joke. It is heavy. Maybe it's supposed to be that way. Maybe having a child is overwhelming by design, because it causes us to look to our true Father who holds us and ours.

You hear so many stories from folks about their experiences in learning the parenting ropes that you don't know exactly what to expect when you get there. We carefully loaded our baby in the car seat, and I drove home with more caution than I had ever driven with before.

As we got settled into the new lifestyle, it was blissful. Ainsley was an amazing, easy baby. She slept through the night quickly and easily. Bedtime was a breeze. We thought, *Man... we are good parents. We have this thing down pat. What is everyone else doing wrong?*

When the next baby came a year later and screamed for months and refused to sleep through the night, our new-parent-fantasyland was shut down. Nevertheless, we were every bit as excited when C.J. arrived as we were with the first. It was falling in love all over again.

I was amazed at how quickly I noticed differences in personality, demeanor, and behavior between the two babies. If you have parented, you know they truly are their own person. We can shape and nurture personalities, but at the end of the day, God has given each one a unique nature.

C.J. was born two months before 9/11. At that time, I still had my full-time job with Delta and the terrorist attacks really rocked the industry. Very few were flying in the months that followed. Delta began shutting jobs down in Dallas and relocating as many as they could to their home base in Atlanta. A supervisor informed me that I too was on the list to be relocated to Georgia. I was freaking out. I didn't want to leave Dallas, but at the same time, I had mouths to feed. The part-time role as junior high youth pastor wasn't enough to anchor us in Dallas.

Vanessa encouraged me to talk to Pastor Terry, so I did. I explained the situation and how much I hated the thought of leaving the area. He offered encouragement and summarized it all by saying, "Trust the Lord. He has it all under control."

I went back to Vanessa.

"What did Terry say?" she inquired.

"He said we are gonna die and that we aren't going to make it."

"No. He didn't. Go talk to him again."

Truth be told, I was filtering all of his encouragement through my own gloom and doom mindset. Pastor Terry was speaking, but fear was translating the message before it got to me. I went back to him. His wisdom didn't change.

"God is on the throne. He loves you. Trust Him. His plan will work out."

He has always maintained that if we keep our hearts pure and truly want to hear from God, we cannot miss Him. Even if we make a mistake or misstep, He is big enough to correct our course and get us back in business. His words settled me.

Delta's plan to relocate me was delayed, and eventually I left employment there anyway when I was offered to come onboard as the full-time junior high school youth pastor at the church. It was a thrilling season. This meant more time with Pastor Terry, being mentored and developed. It meant more time cutting my teeth in the pulpit, more pastoral care, and more involvement in the day-to-day operations of ministry.

I love pastoring. I love the people. If you don't love people, you won't love pastoring. In those early years, I was introduced to pastoral care and what it meant to show up for the flock. I jumped at the chance to do hospital visits, officiate funerals and weddings, and be there for folks in their most vulnerable hour. Terry wanted me to experience these things and I wanted to, as well. They were things they didn't teach me in Bible school. There was no guidebook or lecture on what to do when a family has experienced a suicide and you must show up to their house to walk through the aftermath with them.

I have worked every job in the church except accounting and all of them had a special place. I enjoyed the executive pastor role, preaching and running operations. I loved the growth of the janitorial season and the challenge of maintaining middle schoolers' attention for more than 10 minutes. They have all, in one way or another, helped to build me. As the new millennium progressed, I was leading teens in the church and leading my family at home.

By September of 2002, the birth of our next boy Luke meant we were outnumbered. Vanessa and I had to switch from *one-on-one* to *zone defense*. By this time, Ainsley was a little more independent, so we didn't feel like we were drowning completely. Just drowning a little.

Luke was full of life. Our hearts melted, and we were in awe of how much richer and fuller life felt with little ankle biters running around the house. When the kids were really little, I was working a lot. I do regret the way I tended to fast-forward through some of those seasons.

As a parent, it's easy to bite your nails and tap your feet, waiting impatiently for the baby to sleep through the night. Then you wait for them to be able to feed themselves. Then you want to rush them out of diapers. After that, you are speedily trying to get them to tie their own shoes. Before you know it, you look back and realize you didn't pause to savor any of it. My humble advice? *Slow down.*

Vanessa and I have had a number of conversations about parenting over the years. Fairly early on, we developed our philosophy and approach, tweaking it as needed along the way. Some say, "Kids don't come with an instruction manual." Which is true, but at the same time, the Word of God is even better than an instruction manual—because the Author of the manual Himself is present to help along the way.

We want to bring up children who know *who they are* and *whose they are*. Pam Leo said, "Let's raise kids who don't have to recover from their childhood." I knew I could borrow from the positives of my childhood and bring those things to the table and Vanessa could do the same. For instance, our kids grew up memorizing Scripture, but at the same time, we weren't in the living room for intercession at 5:30 a.m. I wanted them to view the Bible as a *delight,* not a *duty.*

Three kids seemed like a solid number and I was content with that. Vanessa wasn't done though. I explained to her that we weren't having any more children and she objected.

"The Lord told me we are supposed to have four kids."

She just had to bring the Lord into this.

"Not with me!" I responded.

Both of us being double-teamed by these kids? *No, thank you.*

Not long after the discussion, I was in prayer. I figured I would have a conversation with God, since He had supposedly been giving my wife these crazy ideas. He informed me that He did, in fact, speak to her and that we would be having four kids.

I hung up with God and dialed Vanessa. She picked up the phone. I was crying.

"You're right, honey. God spoke to me. We are supposed to have another baby."

By the end of 2003, I was in ministry and loving it with a glowing wife and growing family. We had three babies under three with the last one just a couple months away from being born. It would be the last delivery for Vanessa. What only God knew at the time was that I would be dangerously close to missing it.

CHAPTER EIGHT

THE SHOT

I woke up with a sense of dread before my feet hit the floor that particular morning. I had no natural reason for it, but I also could not deny my apprehension to get the day started. But why? Did I have a bad dream? *No.* Was I going to attend a funeral? *No.*

What was wrong with me?

It was as though I was grieving a loss that hadn't yet happened. Somehow, I was mourning an unknown happening. In fact, the heaviness was so severe I just wanted to stay in bed. It was a gorgeous, unusually warm November day, but I had no desire to leave the house. The weirdness of this was compounded by the fact that I was slated to attend a pastoral retreat in Athens, Texas, that evening—a retreat that I loved going on annually. The main course was deer hunting with a side of *strategic planning.*

A member of the church owned a sizable 2,000-acre ranch and would open its doors yearly to a number of us pastors for rest and relaxation. This Anderson

County property was 20 miles from the nearest town and bordered Catfish Creek, a stream that was rife with alligators, ducks, and fish.

With so many deer, bobcats, and other game on the ranch, the trip was a mixture of clerical comradery and critter control. It is a different type of sanctuary out there. It's a sort of therapy; a reset. The ranch is outfitted with an artesian well onsite that brings up water in a continual flow 24 hours a day, 7 days a week, every day of the year. It's almost prophetically significant, reminding us of the refreshment that's available in that holy ground.

We had already gone down ahead of time to clean up and cut down growth to prepare the hunting blinds and shooting windows. The retreat had been an annual event since the church had started, and mentally, I saw no reason to not go again. But I was in turmoil. Vanessa noticed my state.

"Are you sick? You love to hunt. You should get up and go."

The wariness lingered just enough to sustain my second guessing, but I figured I was just having some irrational response to the plans. I got up, packed up my bags, gun, and gear, and headed out. I picked up a couple of the other pastors on the way. By the time we started spitballing about the hunt and the type of deer we might see, I had forgotten all about any hesitation I had felt that morning.

Vanessa, though, did not forget the hesitation. She continued to pray for me throughout the day—not knowing how valuable that would be.

The plan for the retreat was straightforward. We would wake well before legal shooting light, get to our stands, watch the sunrise over Texas, and hunt our respective blinds until 9:30 a.m. or so. We each had designated blinds with maps and waypoints that would prevent anybody from wandering or being out of place. Everyone knew where everyone would be. We wanted safety, not surprises.

Once back at camp, after the morning hunt, we would have a big breakfast, then meet, talk, share, and pray. After a holy nap, we'd grab sandwiches at 2 p.m. and head back out to the blinds until dark. The night would be punctuated by supper, prayer, talks at the campfire, and hopefully some field dressing from the day's bounty. All was right in the world as the 10 of us pastors arrived at the ranch.

Over the years, hogs began showing up more and more and became a big part of the hunt. Since the introduction of feral hogs to Texas in the 1930s, their population has skyrocketed. These pigs are not a friendly bunch. They do $52 million in damage to the landscape yearly.[2] These wild pigs are generally night creatures, so hunts after sundown became a part of the ordeal.

As we all sat around the campfire that first evening, you couldn't help but take in the beauty of the setting. The stars and the moon were shining in a way that you simply cannot fully appreciate in the city. Open sky country has a way of illuminating and enlarging the cosmos. The weather was also ideal, not too warm and not too cold.

We had just finished eating as Pastor Terry gave us

the details on what to expect during the week. Following that, some went to bed and some lingered in conversation. With an early hunt scheduled for the morning, I decided I should probably turn in for the night.

"I'm headed up to the cabin," I announced. "See you in the morning."

I hopped on the four-wheeler and took off. Earlier that evening, I had gotten into an argument with a close buddy. This disruption was more costly than I could have realized. I was heated over the situation and figured I should pray to figure out what was bothering me.

Instead of meeting with God at the cabin, I took a detour that led to the lake. It wasn't where I said I would be, but that didn't matter to me at the time—everyone else would be in bed soon anyways. I pulled into a quiet spot tucked between the lake and an embankment and shut off the four-wheeler's engine. I had no lights on, the moon was a bright enough lamp for me. The weather was so gorgeous and mild I was comfortable in a black short-sleeved shirt. A harmony of crickets and frogs accompanied my quiet prayers, which were mostly thanksgiving and awe.

I thanked God for the day, for my life, for my family. I thanked Him for the closeness I have always felt with Him when in nature. I had a genuine sense of gratitude for the peace I was soaking up at that very moment.

Before long, the sound of the outdoors was interrupted by the noise of a Kawasaki 4x4 mule, driven by a couple guys from camp. I figured they were headed to the cabin for bed, so I continued to pray, but the noise of the vehicle got louder as they approached. I looked up at the top of the hill and saw their lights. They parked and quietly got out.

With 100 yards between us, it had not occurred to me that they would be out hunting. There had been reports of a massive hog in the area, and they were after him. At 400-plus pounds and wearing all black, the notion of a fatal mix-up should have gotten my attention, but it didn't. Instead, I naively wondered, *Why are they coming over here?*

They shined a light in my direction. With open sights on the rifle, and no thermals or binos, they lacked the magnification they needed to accurately assess their target. Had I known I was, in fact, their target, I would have fired up the four-wheeler and shouted until I went hoarse, but I didn't feel I was in danger at all. In fact, I heard one of them utter reassuring words.

"Do you see him?" he said.

Great, I thought. *They see me, they know I'm down here. No problem.*

I even gave them a friendly wave.

The next words weren't so comforting.

"Shoot!"

The fateful trigger was pulled. The firing pin tapped on the small primer, igniting the 25 grains of flammable gunpowder that sat waiting in the cartridge. Things were in motion that could not be undone. That small, controlled explosion had its way and out from the barrel came a .762 hollow point round with nothing to stop it but my body.

Because an AK-47 round travels twice as fast as the speed of sound, I technically felt the shot before I heard it... but make no mistake: I heard it. It was the loudest, most piercing sound I have had the displeasure of experiencing. The energy, the whistling of the bullet, the muzzle blast—it was deafening. And unfortunately, more bullets were on their way. It was a nightmarish symphony of four rounds in succession.

The first blew a hole in my left side and came out my right. The hollow-point did its job, which was to destroy everything in its path. As the round broke apart and spread out, it sliced, ripped, and burned a horrific hole through my torso. My screaming might have gotten their attention, had it not been masked by the sound of another blast from the muzzle.

The next shot lodged in my right arm, near my bicep. By this time, only a second had elapsed. I began falling off the side of the four-wheeler I was perched on. A third shot was dispersed, and the bullet whistled past my head. How close it was, I'll never know—nor do I want to. The fourth and final round came to a stop when it hit the rim of the ATV.

The metallic ding and unmistakable spark signaled to the pair that it was time to stop shooting. Something had gone wrong. The serenity I felt moments earlier was now history. I do not know which came first, the burning pain or the chilling fear, but neither one delayed their arrival.

I hit the ground hard. Blood quickly formed a river down my arm. With both an entry and exit wound in my midsection, blood spilled from both sides of me. It was not trickling but gushing. I didn't have time to consider the internal hemorrhaging, but it was happening rapidly.

I tried to take a breath, but the air wouldn't come. My diaphragm was in a state of temporary paralysis. The wind was knocked out of me. I panicked for air and finally could gasp in a breath. I didn't curiously remark, "Something bit me," like Forrest Gump after he was shot. I did not gracefully fall to the ground covering my entry wound in slow motion. I was a bleeding, blithering mess. Make no mistake, these accidents are ugly.

It would have been a good time for adrenaline to kick in and mask the pain, but it seemed that all the adrenal hormone in the world wasn't going to take away the burning, stabbing, shooting excruciation I was feeling.

It took them less than a minute to make the 100-yard trek to my location. They ran up, completely oblivious to what happened, and asked, "Where's the hog?"

"You shot me!" I screamed.

Those words hit them like returned fire. They stepped closer and saw my state. When they registered what had happened, it was a panicked frenzy. I was screaming uncontrollably and nearly nonstop. It was the only thing that brought a slight sense of relief.

One of the men hopped back in the 4X4 and drove off to get immediate help. The man who had pulled the trigger stayed with me. Instantly he was weeping, crumbled and helpless. That made two of us. I was blood-soaked from head to toe and began setting my affairs in order.

I knew I was not dead. Reason being, I was in too much pain to be dead. Yet I was pretty sure death was coming. Each breath became more and more labored. There was no tourniquet available and even if there was, it was useless on a torso wound. My life did not flash before my eyes, but my family did.

I mustered up the oxygen I could and spoke what I believed to be my final words.

"I'm not going to make it. I won't live through this. You have to tell Vanessa that I love her. Tell her it was an accident and I'm so sorry this happened. Tell her I'm sorry I won't be able to do life with her."

I was as sincere as a human could possibly be. Nothing meant more than for him to relay my heart to my own.

"Tell Ainsley that Daddy is sorry I won't be able to see her graduate and walk her down the aisle. I'm sorry I can't be there for all the things I promised."

My words were forced out between pants, gasps, and shouts of agony.

"Tell C.J. that I'm sorry I won't be able to see him grow up and play football with him. Tell Luke that Daddy is sorry he's not going to be there. Make sure you tell him I love him and want the absolute best for him."

There was one more.

"Tell my unborn child that I'm so sorry I won't be able to be there. I need all of my kids to know how much I love them and how sorry I am. Please tell them that I'll be cheering them on from heaven."

He did not answer with, "I promise I will," like I expected. His response was more faith-fueled than that.

"*You* are going to tell them, Chris!"

He was picking up on a miracle that I was nowhere near certain of. Fear was pouring into me as quickly as the blood was pouring out of me. Yet I did have a sense of peace after I had left that message for my wife and children. At least I was not going to die alone. I had some sense of closure.

It was silent for several minutes while we waited for help.

When word got back to the camp, I was later told it was full blown pandemonium. No one was prepared for it. How could they be? An ambulance was obviously called, and first responders were in motion.

The men at the camp had heard the shots but couldn't have imagined where those bullets were winding up. The foreman of the ranch lived next door and was a first responder himself, so when the ambulance arrived, he was able to direct them through the property. However, they still had a 20-minute drive out to the middle-of-nowhere to get me. In the meantime, a couple of the pastors drove a truck back to my location to get me up and into an easier pick-up zone.

The man who had gone back to get help was now onsite with the absolute smallest elder that Sojourn Church had on staff, and they were tasked with picking up 416 pounds of dead weight and placing me in the back of the truck.

"Alright, we have to try to get him in," one of them directed. "We need a guy on each arm and someone to grab his feet."

They scrambled into position. They managed to lift

me slightly off the dirt only to drop me seconds later. The ground was unforgiving. The pain continued to mount. They reassessed, repositioned, and lifted me again. With no grip and little strength, they dropped me a second time. By that point, I had had enough.

"Stop! Stop! Stop! Just let me die. Please let me die here!"

I meant it.

The small elder heard my request and leaned down to my ear.

"Chris, we have the truck here, but we cannot pick you up. If you are going to get help, you have got to get up and get into the truck. We can't do it without your help."

As I laid there, it was almost a laughable thought. I chewed on what he said. *Does he know the condition I am in? I've been shot! And I'm supposed to stand up and hop in the bed of the truck?* As stark as reality was, he was right. I had to help myself. Either I would die by that lake or get up and have a fighting chance.

Through the most intense pain of my life, by the grace of God, I stood up with my hands over my wounds and threw myself into the bed of the truck. I was many miles and many prayers from being in the clear, but I was now mobile. My tranquility by the lake had turned to trauma in the most severe way and the clock was ticking.

CHAPTER NINE

THE RUSHED RIDE

Every man thinks he is tougher than a three-dollar steak until he's tossed around in a truck bed with a bullet wound in his gut. It goes without saying that the backroads of a Texas ranch are not smoothly designed for transporting gunshot victims. Ruts, game trails, and holes from hogs meant that my temporary ambulance, a Ford F-150, was being thrown around the dirt path like a rag doll. Every jolt felt like someone was sticking a knife in my wound and twisting the blade. I can still hear the sound of the exhaust and the rattling of the truck with every bump.

The drive felt like an eternity. The vehicle's suspension did not seem to be doing me any favors as I would wail with every rock and sway. As I was tossed around, I couldn't help but think, *Are they looking for potholes? Going out of their way to hit them?*

Sitting next to me in the back of the truck was a man named John, who was fervently praying in the Spirit over me. An almost indescribable sense came over me that I was all right with God. Paul spoke in Romans 5:1 of our peace with God through Jesus, and in those moments, it was more real to me than ever. I figured I would make my leap to glory any minute, and I found myself surprisingly content with that. Having peace with God eased the transition. *Perhaps the Lord wanted me to get myself up off the ground so no one would have to lift my dead body into the truck*, I thought. It was my final generous contribution to the Sojourn staff—a parting gift, if you will.

It was time to turn out the lights. Twenty-six years was a shorter go at this thing than I had expected, but there was nothing more that could be done about that. *Okay, Lord,* I thought. *I'm ready.*

In full disclosure, I had never died prior to this. As a pastor, I've been with a number of people as they passed peacefully into heaven, but no one had informed me on how to actually go about it. I was new to the process. I decided I would try the ultra-spiritual route. When Jesus gave up His life, He prayed a specific prayer. If it worked for Him on the cross, it would work for me on the truck bed. I closed my eyes and prayed.

"Lord, I'm ready. Into Thy hands I commit my spirit."

The prayer was carried to heaven in the sincerest King James-speak that I could muster. Yet for some reason, it didn't work. I opened one eye. Sure enough, I was still in the back of the truck. Perhaps I had not said it correctly. Maybe I just needed to mimic the persistent widow and do it again.

"Lord," I prayed, "into *Thy* hands, I commit my spirit."

God did not answer my prayer, but He *responded* to my prayer. Often, our prayers don't need an answer. They need a *response* instead. What's the difference? Answered prayer is a fulfillment of our desire. It's when we get what we asked for. However, when God *responds to* a prayer, it means He may speak back with a solution that's better than what we had in mind originally. God is known to reject the prayers we are *currently* praying to answer the prayers we *should* be praying. In this case, He did just that.

Immediately after I said those words, God responded. Not by bringing me to heaven, but by bringing heaven to me. Suddenly, every prayer that my mother ever prayed over me began flooding into my heart. In a flash, I remembered every time somebody laid hands on me when I was a kid to pray and speak life over me. I began to recall all the Scripture verses I memorized.

A flood of prophetic words that had been spoken over me began cycling through my heart and mind. Pastor Terry had told me that he did not see me being just a youth pastor, but that I would be used to teach and preach in bigger ways. I believed him when he told me this in church and I believed him when it came back to mind in the back of that truck.

All of the dreams and promises that I had as a husband, a father, and as a leader in the church were rushing into my spirit like rapids. I knew there were still promises not yet fulfilled. There was vision that had not been exhausted. I was not finished yet. Faith swelled in my heart and a supernatural peace blanketed me. I started speaking to myself like a wild man.

"I am not done. I've got stuff to do. There are things God has called me to, and I'm not finished yet. My God is all-powerful, an all-consuming fire. Greater is He who is inside of me than He who is in the world. I've got a family waiting for me. I am *not* going to die. I am going to live. It ain't over."

I closed my self-talk by an optimistic decree over my wounds, "They are not that bad."

When I opened my eyes and looked down, they were *that bad*. However, my spirit was still in agreement with the prayers and promises over my life. What I saw in my heart was greater than the damage I was seeing in my physical body. It was bad, and frankly, it could have gotten worse, but I was still fully persuaded that I would live. There was no undoing this newfound, crunch time revelation.

———

A devastatingly hard phone call had to be made that night to Vanessa. One of the pastors at the retreat named Mike dialed and dropped the bomb. "Chris has been shot." It did not strike Vanessa as being reality. He was known for being a jokester, so she brushed it off. Perhaps I had put him up to it. When no laugh or relief came from the end of the line, she knew it was serious.

"Vanessa, you know I would never joke about something like this. I'll call you back when I know more."

As things developed, he rang her again. She had a couple questions. First, "Who shot Chris?"

When Mike told her, her heart sank. Reason being, the week before I had gone out with that very pastor to buy the very gun that was used. In fact, I distinctly told Vanessa, "It's more gun than he needs, definitely over-kill, but it's a good one."

She knew the gun. She knew the caliber. She knew the damage. That revelation lent itself to her next question.

"Do we have life insurance?"

Fear did not waste time trying to make an entry. At the time, she did not have the faith to believe I would make it. The fatality rates are too high in these situations. She began to pray. Strange as it might sound, when Vanessa needs comfort, her go-to is not necessarily to seek out a mentor or find a shoulder to cry on. Instead, she takes a bath. It's her prayer closet. Some take walks, others take drives—Vanessa takes baths. We all need refuge, and this just happens to be her source of distraction-free grace at the feet of Jesus. She was soaking in the tub and soaking in prayer. During that time, a faith rose in her and she knew things would somehow be okay.

Upon hearing about the incident, Mike's wife wanted to come to the house to be with her, but she drew the line and did not want visitors. She found strength and peace in her own personal sanctuary.

When my parents were called, my father broke down. Also being well-seasoned with firearms, he knew what a .762 round could do to a body. Yet their prayers for me had begun before their phone ever rang with the news. Their church had been participating in a forty-day fast, focused around praying for the children. For weeks leading up to the incident, my folks had been covering me with prayer daily. Prayers of protection had gone up before I was ever knocked off the four-wheeler.

Whether you are aware or not, people are praying for you. Perhaps it's your own parents or grandparents. It could be the case that you have no relative or close friend praying. If that's the case, rest assured that Jesus is praying for you (see Hebrews 7:25). Beyond that, I have prayed for everyone who hears or reads my story, and that includes you.

Prayer is the ladle that allows us to dip into the river of God, drinking in His grace, insight, protection, wisdom, and help. It changes everything. The true movers and shakers on this planet are not the tycoons and billionaires. They are the prayer warriors. It's those who live on their knees. In fact, this divinely timed season of prayer and fasting back in Arkansas may be the reason I am still on the planet.

Upon hearing the news, my parents had dozens of members in their church lifting me up along with them. While still in transit in the back of the truck, prayer chains grew like vines, spiritually wrapping me up. The jostling finally ceased as we came to a stop at the highway entrance to the property where we would meet the ambulance. I might not have been completely out of the weeds, but thank God I was no longer on pothole alley.

There, I saw Pastor Terry. He, too, was praying for me. I looked around and noticed several other pastors praying for me likewise.

The ambulance had made its way to us and the first responders began prepping the stretcher. It was a chaotic situation. We were trying to stop the bleeding while also trying to manage the pain. When I again heard the sound of Pastor Terry praying for me, I tried to talk to him, but the words weren't coming out right. He approached me.

"Son..."

It was the most comforting sound I had heard in my 26 years of life.

"Are you okay?" He took off his jacket and placed it under my head. There were lots of folks there praying who were genuinely concerned. Yet it was the heart of my spiritual father who not only prayed, but went the extra mile to place a cushion under my head. It was an act of service that had *spiritual dad* written all over it.

Hearing his voice brought comfort in the midst of all the screaming, shouting, and pandemonium. While nothing could stop the bleeding and the pain, the prayers of Pastor Terry, the group, Vanessa, my parents, and the growing prayer chain made all of the difference. While first responders were doing what they could to bring relief, prayer was all that we had to lean on.

Corrie ten Boom famously said, "You may never

know that Jesus is all you need, until Jesus is all you have." Bleeding out at a ranch in rural Texas left me and all of the prayer warriors with nothing but Jesus and Jesus alone.

Figuring out how to get someone my size with multiple gunshot wounds from a truck to an operating room table before bleeding out was no small task. The paramedics adjusted the stretcher to match the truck hitch height and wheeled it over. From there, they were tasked with the move. In time, they maneuvered me onto the gurney.

It had been about an hour-and-a-half since I had been shot, and the muscles on the side of my body were violently spasming. My body knew this gaping hole was not supposed to be there, and my nerve endings reacted by twitching in an attempt at putting my flesh back together.

Not long after, my entire body began shaking also. The pain was now graduating from a steady burning to a terrorizing stabbing sensation that pulsed with every beat of my heart. While some clotting was taking place, I was still losing ample amounts of blood. The light-headedness from this and the trauma in general had me phasing in and out of consciousness.

Before we got going, the paramedics phoned into the nearby hospital to alert them of our arrival. The small hospital then informed the paramedics that they were not outfitted to care for a gunshot victim. They resolved to take me to a larger city about twice as far away. To do so efficiently, a helicopter was called.

This meant more waiting.

Which meant more blood loss.

In the meantime, I was begging for pain relief. One of the three paramedics tied off my arm and had me squeeze a ball in an attempt to find a vein. Pain meds seemed to be on their way. The first responders were encircling my body like a flock of vultures over roadkill, grabbing this and prepping that. I kept my eyes closed for much of the process but when I did open, I saw a blur of anxious activity. In the midst of hands reaching over me, vitals being read, and medical jargon being spoken from one to the other, a paramedic looked at me and said, "Mr. McRae, we cannot find a vein."

Without an IV, I was left to manage the pain myself. One of the paramedics had an unorthodox idea: "I know there's a vein under his toenail—let's go through the nail to access it."

I had already had a couple of unwelcomed holes created in my body that night. I didn't need another through my toenail, for God's sake. The goal was to take away my pain, not create more of it. I was about to tell them to stay away from my feet when a voice came over their radios asking about my predicament.

"Have you given him pain meds?" the voice inquired.

"No. Trying to but can't find a vein."

"*Do not* give him *anything* for pain."

This was devastating. Sorrow upon sorrow. Going in and out of consciousness offered marginal relief, but not nearly enough given my plight. The rationale was that the hospital needed me to be fully awake upon arrival. Sedation was not an option. Beyond that, they did not know the full extent of the damage done to my abdomen. It was possible that medication could have done more long-term harm than short-term good—something they did not want to risk.

As I approached two hours of living with a hole in both sides, I spasmed, shook, writhed, and fought. I was fighting for much more than relief. I was fighting for my future and my family. Optimism does not come easy to someone filled with bullet shrapnel. Yet the goodness and glory of the gospel remained the same—whether I was on a bloody gurney or in a safe, warm bed at home.

When the word came that I needed to be airlifted to Tyler, I was driven to an open field in front of the main house. The men lined up vehicles around the perimeter to light the landing area for the helo. I was fairly oblivious to the whole ordeal. Not long after, in the distance, I heard the faintest sound of a beating drum. It was subtle, but I couldn't miss it. It grew louder and louder, coming to a crescendo.

"What's that noise?"

"Mr. McRae, that's the helicopter. It's coming to get you."

I was overjoyed. This news hit me with hope. It was the sound of my rescue. In Vietnam, the UH-1H Helicopter, nicknamed "Huey" picked up soldiers to carry them to safety. Its super distinct sound was known as "the sound of freedom." While I had not been picked up on a battlefield, I was certainly being picked up in dire straits. Because of this, I can forever relate to the relief of *the sound of freedom.*

CHAPTER TEN

UNDER THE KNIFE

The propellers introduced high speed winds into camp as the helo slowly landed. It was time to switch vehicles. A crew emerged from the aircraft, already thoroughly briefed on my situation. The paramedics were probably more than ready to hand me off. I was someone else's problem at that point.

"What's your weight, Mr. McRae?"

Being 416 pounds at the time, they had some adjustments to make inside the helicopter. Both the flight and ambulance crew were all hands on deck to help make the transition to the inside of the aircraft. Traumatized and exhausted, I was just happy to be leaving the ranch.

Like an elevator in motion, I felt us lifting off. We were bound for Tyler, Texas. Time was a blur. Was everything happening incredibly fast or in super slow motion? I couldn't tell. I was worn out beyond comprehension and decided to close my eyes for a moment. I did not close them all the way, though; just enough so I could still see the helicopter paramedics to my right and left. As I lay there with my eyes barely open, I noticed one of them take his hand and slice his fingers in a wave across his neck. It was the universal sign for "this fella just died."

"Hey!" I shouted. "What did you do that for?!"

Slightly embarrassed and slightly stunned, he said, "Mr. McRae, you stopped talking to us."

"Well, what do you want to talk about? We can talk about anything you want! How 'bout them Cowboys?"

News, weather, politics, sports—I was ready to chat. Being presumed dead was not exactly comforting to witness, and I was not about ready for them to pull the blanket over my face. My eyes were wide open from then on out.

It was a 20-minute escort to the hospital and proved to be smoother than the backcountry truck ride. My pastor and a couple others hopped in trucks and drove to be there for my arrival. What I had not computed at the time was that this was a precarious situation for my pastor friends.

Just a few years prior to this, a black man had been killed and dragged around by a group of white men in Jasper, Texas—just a couple hours away. When word got out to authorities that a black man had been shot at a retreat amongst a bunch of white men, it raised eyebrows. So not only did an ambulance show up, but a man with a badge did, too. He had some questions and rightfully so. The pastor who had shot me was not white himself, but it still drew attention. In fact, they took him for questioning at the Athen's Sheriff's office. Fortunately, the elder who told me I needed to stand up and get in the truck was an attorney as well, and went to the Sheriff's office with him. He was able to dismiss accusations, explain the negligence, and stifle investigation with some key conversations. I was later told he was there until 5 a.m. keeping the pastor from being arrested. Had he not been there, there may have been a few men booked that night until further investigation was done.

After touchdown on the hospital pad and after being wheeled into the hospital, I imagined an emergency operating room, swarming with nurses, anesthesiologists, and doctors, like bees in a hive. The movies always portray well-choreographed chaos with phrases floating through the air like, "Clear the area," and "I need 22 CC's of tramadol, stat!"

This wasn't the case as I was wheeled back to the O.R. Instead, the first question I heard was from one worker to another: "What'd you have for dinner, Ralph?"

Ralph had a Hungry-Man T.V. dinner.

I was a little put off by the banter. It was my *life* we were dealing with, after all. To them, it was another day at work. I, of course, wanted undistracted urgency and focus. But, as long as the doctor who was cutting me open wasn't chewing on a Salisbury steak and talking about his upcoming golf trip, I was okay.

As the two workers wheeled me into the room, the doctor and nursing staff awaited me. It was completely white, floor to ceiling with bright fluorescents illuminating every square inch of the operating room. The entire crew donned white scrubs. A tray filled with scalpels, tweezers, forceps, and other instruments was wheeled in.

My shirt was cut off of me and I made my final transition for a while to the operating table. A surgeon standing next to me spoke up and began detailing to the crew just how the surgery would play out. He described where they would make incisions, how they would evaluate the damage, and what the clean-up and patch-up would look like. In the midst of the briefing, I couldn't take it any longer.

I reached up, grabbed onto his white collar, and pulled him down to me.

"Doc... you need to give me something for this pain, *right now.*"

A few in the room snickered. I didn't.

The surgeon smiled, stood up, straightened his collar, and said, "Okay, big boy." An apparatus was placed over my face and anesthetic, in gas form, filled my nostrils. *Finally.* Everything slowed down. I forgot my pain in that split second before drifting off and the agony was over. I was out cold and under the knife.

———

Throughout the surgery, the medical staff called Vanessa to keep her in the loop on my progress. It was the sweetest act of service. Those calls kept going until 4 a.m. when the emergency operation was finally complete. With three kids in bed, loading them up in the middle of the night to drive to a hospital in a different city with a paper map in hand just wasn't an option. It was best to wait until morning.

She was able to snag a couple hours of sleep before making the trip at dawn. A friend who also had small kids agreed to stay at our place with our children. Being so young, Vanessa kept the little ones away from the situation. To them, they had an exciting playdate ahead.

From the early days of dating Vanessa, she had always been *home* to me. She's not just a person, but a place, so to speak. A place to start and a place to end each day. Her warmth and familiar voice have been an anchor throughout our life together. This was exemplified perfectly when I awoke from surgery, wiped the blurriness from my eyes, and saw her concerned gaze staring at me.

My heart nearly exploded with joy, hope, and happiness.

Less than 10 hours earlier, I didn't know if I would ever see her again, yet here we both were. The relief flooded my entire being. Doubtless, the vast majority of people with my wounds would not have made it. I was humbled as this second chance at life was unfolding in front of me. I was going to be able to embrace my loved ones again. I would have tickle fights with my kids again. I would crack jokes to Vanessa again. I would preach again. I was going to *live* again.

I was wrapped up in so many bandages that she thought I was covered in sheets at first. I know that *I love yous* were exchanged and I probably asked how the kids were doing as best I could, considering I had a tube down my throat. Being fairly heavily medicated, the memory remains a blur, but the feeling of it does not. I had been unconscious for several hours after Vanessa's arrival so she was glad to see the whites of my eyes again. Everything was going to be okay. This was not a hollow platitude, but a reality that I felt in my bones. I was going to make it. I was stable.

Right next to Vanessa was my friend. Not just any friend, but the one who had mistakenly pulled that fateful trigger. His face was downturned, staring at his hands. He, I'm sure, felt guilty, downcast, and embarrassed. He had no words. It occurred to me almost instantly that I had words I needed to share with him. As best I could, I spoke and signaled with clapped hands, "I am praying for you." With a face full of medical equipment, it was all I could get out. Yet it was exactly what needed to happen.

Before bitterness had a chance to plant a seed in my heart, I wanted to establish that my soul and spirit would not be a greenhouse for bitterness. Instead, I would be a greenhouse for love, forgiveness, and peace to grow in. Truly, I held no unforgiveness toward him—not then and not now. It was an accident. When I released him, I released me.

Sure, it was unwise to shoot at a target that was not fully identified. Yet it was completely stupid of me to be wearing a black shirt, at night, with no lights on, in front of an embankment that provided me with no silhouette. Beyond that, I was in a different place than I said I would be. My dad reminded me of this when he arrived at the hospital with my mom.

"You know better than to be somewhere other than where you said you'd be, Chris."

"I know."

It was a blessing to see my parents, as sighs of relief were shared all around. My injuries were severe, but recovery was in sight. The bullet that hit my arm lodged deep in my bicep. Miraculously, the hollow point did not expand and did not pass through. Had it done so, it very well could have blown my arm off, frankly. I later joked that it didn't penetrate due to my flexing before it hit. They were able to extract the bullet, which I still have.

The injuries to my torso were not so benign. The medical team had to remove a foot of my intestines that were too damaged to repair. From there, they used internal sutures, cleaned the internal wounds, and removed all the shrapnel they could find. Using a synthetic mesh, they patched up my diaphragm.

Needless to say, I was hitting the morphine button like it was a full-time job. Someone mentioned, "Chris, you know they put a governor on the morphine machine so you can only get so much, right?"

"I don't care. I don't want to miss one second when that next dose comes available."

As I lay in recovery, it occurred to me that I hadn't yet seen the gunshot wound in broad daylight. I had certainly felt it, but had not laid eyes on it. I lifted my head, pulled up my gown and saw a massive, gaping hole in my torso. It was so large that my hand was unable to fully cover it. At the very sight of this I became lightheaded and proceeded to faint. This would take some getting used to.

They left the wound open for the purpose of being able to vacuum it out and cut down on infection. More on that later. To my surprise, the hospital staff wasted no time on recovery. Just a day after the surgery, I was laying in my hospital room when my physical therapy nurse came in. She had a name that fit her stature: Bertha. She was, perhaps, the biggest nurse in Tyler, Texas. I was no fun-sized patient, so the match made sense.

She did not sugar coat nor mince words. With a direct word and a no-nonsense delivery, she informed me that I was going to be getting up to walk.

"No, ma'am. I'm not ready to walk. I've been shot."

"Yes, I know you've been shot. And no, you're not staying in bed. You are getting up."

"No ma'am, I'm staying in this bed," I countered.

"No, sir, you will walk. I'm going to get you up and *you will* take some steps."

"But what about the pain?"

"Here's some ice chips."

I stared at her. I knew she meant business and wasn't going to let me stay in bed. It felt unfair, though. I was the victim, after all. I was the one with a gaping wound. The bed was warm, soft, and comfortable. How was I going to get up, let alone walk?

"I really can't, Bertha. I'm not ready!"

Ready or not, Bertha was getting me up and out of bed. She lowered the side rails and instructed me,

"Move your leg a little in this direction. Now move the other."

"Slowly lower each leg to the ground."

"Grab this rail.

"Take my hand."

With a cocktail mixture of instruction, inspiration, and perhaps a little irritation, Bertha helped me sit up on the bed with feet on the ground. With her help, I stood. Thoroughly humbled through and through, I felt I had done enough.

"Move your leg forward a little."

I took one baby step, exhausted, in pain, and miserable. I was ready to get back in bed when Bertha expressed that she wasn't yet satisfied.

"One more step. Stick your leg out and plant that foot. It's all you need to do, and we'll call it a day."

I did. Through lip biting, sweating, and grimacing, I did.

Bertha helped get me back in bed. Pain came in a fresh wave. There weren't enough drugs in the hospital that could have alleviated the nasty effect of those baby steps. Gravity can be cruel. Every time I stood, my flesh was pulled down and the wound was stretched. I rested for the night and enjoyed the precious visits of loved ones. I embraced my kids the best I could from the bed. Seeing them again was a treasure beyond words. Concerned friends arrived, offered prayer, joked with me, and cheered me up.

The next day, Bertha came back for more therapy. She was relentlessly interested in my recovery. At the time, it felt like she was relentlessly interested in my agony. After lumbering my way to my feet, I did my two baby steps. That's when she pushed me further.

"Can you do more?"

"No."

To this, she responded, "You're going to."

There was no arguing with her, and I knew it. I had tried that plenty, to no avail.

If I could have gotten away with staying in that bed, I would have. Wallowing in my pain and feeling sorry for myself, I would have dwelt on my excuses and made the victim mentality my home—and why shouldn't I? Was I not the victim of a gunshot? Make that multiple gunshots, to be exact. Yet my excuses, as alluring as they might be, would have kept me down and out. Bertha crashed my pity party, cut the music, and turned on the lights. It was time to move.

I took those two steps, and then three more after that. Day two was better than the first. Following my quality time with Bertha, the doctor came to check in.

"Mr. McRae, how are you doing?"

"I'm doing terrible."

"You look it—but you better be glad to be here," he responded. "That was quite an ordeal. You are lucky to be alive."

Not lucky. Luck has nothing to do with the Lord working His plan to protect the purposes of my life, I thought.

With these thoughts left unspoken, he continued to chart the course of recovery.

"The hollow point exploded as it passed through you. We removed a foot of your intestines and washed the area with saline solution to prevent infection. We've left the wound open for daily cleaning."

I nodded. Then he spoke a single line that contained an entire sermon.

"Mr. McRae, in order for this to heal, it needs to happen from the inside out."

He went on to explain the wound vacuum attached to my torso and its purpose in helping to clean and close the wound.

"How long will I have this suction cup?" I inquired.

"As long as it takes."

This would be no short drive. I was in for a long road to recovery. I had no choice.

CHAPTER ELEVEN

FINDING NORMAL

"Are you ready to walk again?" I really wasn't. But I got up anyway. The first week following the incident was an interval of sleep, pushing the morphine button, and grinding out steps with Bertha. Within a couple weeks, I had mounted enough strength and stability to feel ready to climb a few stairs. When that did not topple me, I figured I could climb an entire flight of them.

Each therapy session was punctuated by me collapsing into the bed in a sleepy, exhausted haze. My steady diet of IV fluid and ice chips was not the fuel my body was accustomed to. I finally felt healthy enough to attempt expanding my diet, graduating from ice chips to foods like pudding and oatmeal. Switching to toddler meals was a giant leap for both my system and my morale.

By a few weeks in, I was itching to get home.

"What do I have to do to get out of here, Bertha?"

"When you can walk on your own from your room to the front doors of the hospital, we'll clear you to leave."

That finish line gave me the oomph I needed. Within a couple days, I was walking on my own to those glorious automatic sliding hospital doors. I celebrated my soon departure, making sure Bertha kept her end of the bargain.

I've come to learn that the biggest difference between Bertha and myself was the way our gowns tied. I was the patient whose gown tied in the back. I was the one with the physical trauma that needed to be remedied. I had the issues, bullet fragments, and scar tissue. That back-exposed uniform was my fashion for some time and indicated to everyone that I was the patient, not the professional.

Bertha's scrubs, however, tied in the front. She and the medical team could care for themselves and thus care for me. It's the classic airline instruction, "Put your own oxygen mask on first before helping others." I was in no position to help me. But they were. While much of my recovery was left to my own willingness to stand and push forward, the ultimate directives were given by the medical team.

So often, we want God to pull every lever, press every button, and do all of the recovery for us. Yet He guides it and allows us to participate. For others, though, they want to manage the entire recovery process, excluding

God and His power from it. This also leads to a botched program. Our role in recovery, from anything in life, is to partner with God's directive.

As I locked arms with Bertha in the healing process, I became more stable. I slowly transitioned from being helpless to helping, and eventually, not needing any help at all. Sometimes we need someone to walk with us until we are able to walk on our own. Vanessa would bring the kids to see me during those weeks, which was a huge boost of strength. Having now climbed my own personal Mount Everest (walking to the hospital entrance), it was time to enjoy my victory from the comforts of home. It was time to trade my gown and hospital footies for my own clothes again.

Making my way outside to the carport after being discharged was uplifting, to say the least. Breathing fresh air, after weeks in a hospital room, was balm for the soul. I wish I could say that recovery got easier with each day, but the days turned to weeks and those weeks turned to months of hospital stays, doctor visits, and constant physical pain. In retrospect, I see that I should have stayed in the hospital longer. I was a lot of work for Vanessa, even with a nurse coming daily. I basically lived in a recliner for a year because it was easy in, easy out.

I also could not be alone for long. When Vanessa would run to the grocery store, she would have someone watch me. Being babysat was a new experience. I brought it on myself though, because on the first or second day home, I had thrown up into a bowl. Not wanting to burden Vanessa, I tried to get up by myself to go dump it. On my way to the bathroom, I passed out and hit the ground. Vanessa later found me and was tasked with getting me and my vomit off the floor. Boy, I had taken my independence for granted prior to the accident.

When a follow-up procedure was needed, I was back in the hospital to go under the knife. Friends would come visit while I was recovering from yet another surgery, but few of them could stomach the reality of how bad things were. In fact, on one occasion a friend actually passed out from seeing the wound. A gunshot hole, in reality, is not quite like they appear in movies. They're awful. And I can testify that they feel worse than they look.

A short while after the accident, Vanessa went into labor with our fourth and final child. I was very weak during the birth, so I laid on the couch in the delivery room. Vanessa warned the nurses that she was very close to being ready. They lollygagged and figured it would be a while yet. Of course, this was not her first rodeo; they should have listened. When from the couch I yelled, "The head is out!" they scrambled and got into position.

At least I contributed something.

It was the 29th of January, 2004, and our girl Braiden made her way into our world and our hearts. We were enamored and in awe, per usual. This time, though, I couldn't help Vanessa to recover, as I was recovering, as well. In fact, the morning after Braiden was born, I was in the same hospital having a procedure done. Fortunately, Vanessa's mom was in from New Hampshire to carry responsibilities that I could not.

The appointments, visits, and evaluations seemed constant. On one such appointment, I was to see a surgeon who would remove the bandages and examine my wounds. The dressings at this time were not made up of a little layer of gauze pads and medical tape. No, my core was *completely* wrapped up with thick dressing and reinforcements.

You can imagine my and Vanessa's shock when the surgeon did not know how to put the dressings back on after taking a look. In fact, he actually said, "You know how to put this back on, right?"

No. We did not.

We went to Bible school, not medical school. It was yet another reminder that the damage caused by these shots was beyond what most doctors had seen and treated before. I was in a "special category" of trauma patients.

As time wore on, multiple surgeries took place to repair the extent of the damage. With each surgery, it seemed new problems were revealed. Two of the surgeries were hernia related. Others involved fixing up staples and sutures. Some were to clean up scar tissue and others were to repair the hernia mesh used to keep my insides on the inside. Lots of bullet fragments and foreign matter also surfaced as years passed.

In total, it took roughly seven months to be at a place of moderate normalcy, working and functioning again. A total of six surgeries would occur in the years that followed the incident.

My focus in the early months had been dialed in on repairing and healing the *physical* wounds. I was eager to return to the life I had before absorbing bullets. Yet I took emotional blasts that night which had flown under the radar for some time. I genuinely had no clue how severe the psychological trauma was until I began having nightmares. One after another, I would wake up drenched and panting. My times of rest were disrupted by brutal torment.

I knew how to treat the physical pain. I had medication for that. I knew what I could handle and what I could not. Yet for the nightmares, they seemed to consume my mind and I needed an answer. I called the man who is always in my corner.

"Pastor Terry, I don't know what's going on. I'm having nightmares all the time. I can't shake them."

Without the slightest hesitation, he diagnosed it.

"That's trauma."

He instantly identified the spiritual attack. You cannot *eliminate* what you do not first *illuminate*, and Pastor Terry had certainly illuminated what was ailing my mind. He continued, "You've got to take control and authority over the trauma that has entered your life." It was more than just praying for a speedy physical healing. I needed the darkness over my mind removed also. The enemy is an opportunist who will attach himself to areas of trauma and weakness.

Right then over the phone, my pastor prayed for me. It was the most sincere prayer. God freed me, once and for all, that day. The tight grip of fear that kept me mentally paralyzed was lifted. My mind and my night seasons were free, and free indeed.

While my mind was at rest and the nightmares gone, the physical pain was not instantly lifted. For many months, I dealt with excruciating pain that would come and go. I had trouble moving and felt sad and irritable. I also wrestled with feeling bummed that my family had to deal with all of this. My pain was causing them pain, as well. A nurse came to our home every day to make sure I was healing okay and to monitor medication doses.

The pain meds certainly helped, but after some time, I realized that I was taking the highest doses that they could offer me. Morning and night, pills were being popped. It's not as though I was taking medicine in vain. I needed it. But after seven months of this, I started to get concerned that I might develop a habit, or worse yet, an actual *dependency* on pain medication. Signs were showing that it was becoming a crutch that I leaned on, and even Vanessa was concerned.

Once again, I turned to my spiritual father.

"Pastor Terry, I don't know how to say this, but something is going on," I told him. "I think I'm getting too attached to the medication. I feel like I'm having withdrawals when I don't take it."

I had never been addicted to anything, so I wasn't quite sure how to put my finger on what I was feeling.

I began to open up about this chemical dependency with my wife and pastor. Was I stealing from purses to pay for pills? *No.* Was I sticking up gas stations in order to get cash for opioids? *Of course not.* But we don't have to live on the fringe extremes to be able to recognize that something is not healthy.

Opening the conversation that this was becoming a problem was absolutely essential. Admitting issues is a means of avoiding ongoing bondage. The more I talked about it, the less hold the medication had on me. Secrecy has a way of galvanizing darkness in our lives.

Beyond prescriptions, we self-medicate in a variety of ways. Some hide traumas with food, sex, alcohol, entertainment, porn, or gossip. Any number of things can prove to be addictive when it provides a temporary escape from trauma. The problem is, this temporary escape is actually a long-term holding cell, where trauma only compounds and gets worse.

God Himself freed me and set heavenly boundaries in my relationship to medicine as the recovery unfolded. The initial miracle of my very life being saved was now blossoming and multiplying into miracles ranging from physical recovery to emotional liberty. Yet the miracle story was not finished being written just yet.

———

For many years, even prior to the incident, I had been on a drug for my blood. My pastor found himself reading an article one day and recognized the name of the prescription. The study noted that you *cannot* lose weight, no matter what you try, when on this particular pill. Not only that, but 30,000 people had died from its effects. He called me up.

"Chris, what pill are you taking?"

I told him. He showed me the article and it was legitimate. I instantly got off of that medication and immediately began losing weight. Within an unbelievably short period of time, I lost 120 pounds. This was great for my long-term health. I had a new lease on life. I was emotionally and physically free. There was a certain ease to life at that point. I was back in regular ministry and enjoying my role at the church. Appointments to the doctor were few and far between—things were stabilizing.

The problem was that the hernia mesh inside of me was being impacted by the weight loss. The material shifted and began to fold in on itself. The mesh was originally sized for someone over 400 pounds. Well, that guy did not exist any longer. The rapid weight loss meant that my internal sutures were no longer sized correctly.

So, after three years, the pain came back, and it felt like I had been shot all over again. At first, the pain was throbbing. It then transformed to a stabbing pain, like being prodded internally with an ice pick. At times, it became so intense I went into the closet, held a pillow to my face, and screamed into it to avoid my kids hearing my anguish. It was a remarkable setback that I was facing.

Fed up, I finally went back to see a doctor and they did some x-rays. Those images showed metal bullet fragments that had traveled internally and made a line from one side of my body to the other. Some of those pieces of shrapnel were significant in size. My body was doing what it was designed to do, which in this case, was to push the foreign fragments out. All of the bullet splinters were trying to make their way toward the surface of my body, pushing up against scar tissue and nerves. I had the diagnosis. Unfortunately, I had no solution.

"I'm sorry, Chris, there's nothing we can do to help you," the doctor said.

I was stunned. I could not live this way. My torso was filled with cruel confetti that was trying to escape through my skin... *and they had no solution?* I went to Pastor Terry and told him as much and he encouraged me to go to a different doctor. I did. Yet again, I was given the same line.

"I'm sorry, Mr. McRae, we cannot operate on this wound."

I made the circuit. Six different doctors told me that I was going to have to suck it up and deal with this situation as a part of my life. Surgeon after surgeon informed me that there was simply too much damage on the inside of my body, and that operating would just cause more trauma, weakness, and scar tissue build up.

This could not possibly be my existence.

Even after all God had brought me through, I felt ready to give up all hope.

Thankfully, those who loved me would not allow me to throw in the towel. Each time I came back with a negative response from a doctor, those near me would simply say, "Okay, let's try a new doctor." I'd try again, only to be told the same thing. I would then go home only to hear, "Nope, we are not giving up." The cycle continued and I felt like a pinball being bounced back and forth between optimism and opposition, with no end in sight.

I will say, there are very few things more valuable than having people in your life who refuse to give up on you. Mix and mingle with people who have steely faith, fiery love, and a desire to see you well. When friends are willing to fight for you, it will rub off on you. You will start to fight for yourself. Lock arms with those who are willing to slay giants alongside you and you will find yourself in the promised land as a result.

After pulling out all the stops, I visited the University of Texas Southwestern Medical Center. I was told they were the best of the best and that if they could not help me, then no one could. Much was riding on this visit. Pulling up to the multi-campus facility, I had hope.

The visit itself went much like the others. As the doctor wrapped up evaluations, asked the standard questions, and scribbled on a clipboard, I was eager for an answer.

"Well, doc, what do you have for me?"

"Well, wow, you've been through quite an ordeal," he begins. "But Chris, I'm sorry, we can't operate on you."

My heart sank lower than ever. He went on to explain that I would need to take shots and pain medicine for the rest of my life. The risk associated with an operation like that was just too high. No doctor wanted to touch it. There was little upside for them, and lots of downside. They were not about to roll the dice with these fragments and mesh and potentially wind up with a lawsuit. Of course, I was not after a payday. I was after relief.

Completely deflated, I made my way to the car. I didn't know how I was going to go on this way, but I knew God was still good. He still had good things coming, and I had to grasp that, in spite of what I saw or felt. Sitting in the car in the parking lot, I cried out to God in tears.

"God, I'm so defeated! Surely You didn't bring me this far just to leave me in this place of suffering. I know You didn't do all these things to preserve my life, give my wife back her husband, and my kids back their dad, for me to live in misery like this. I know You told me there were things You wanted me to see and do. Help me, Lord!"

I was beaten down. I was in the twelfth round of a brutal heavyweight bout. Yet I concluded the prayer in faith.

"...I will hold on to Your promises, Lord."

No matter the report of the doctors, the report of the Lord would win the day. If it meant battling pain the rest of my life, I would battle it. Yet I would live and see the glory of the Lord.

CHAPTER TWELVE

THE TEMPLE VICTORY

Many years had passed since the incident. My ongoing journey with pain was always looming in the background, yet I had not given up hope. As I wrapped up a sermon on an ordinary Sunday, God was about to re-embark me on my medical mission.

An older gentleman by the name of Victor Salvino approached me. He looked me in the eye, pointed at me, and in a sort of godfather-like voice, said, "Tomorrow morning, 9 o'clock in the morning, you will get a phone call. Answer it. I've taken care of everything."

This was different than the usual, "Great sermon, pastor. Really needed that," type of chitter chatter you get after a Sunday service. This guy meant business. Without saying anything else, he turned and walked away. It was odd, but I couldn't help but recognize the intentionality behind his words.

He was older. I didn't know him all that well, and frankly, I wasn't positive he knew what he was talking about. *What just happened?* I thought to myself.

Sure enough, the next morning at exactly 9 a.m., my phone rang. It was a surgeon from Baylor Scott & White Medical Center in Temple, Texas. They wanted me to come down as soon as I could. They were going to work on me. My heart leapt. I was ecstatic. I couldn't believe that a surgeon had agreed to help me.

While I was hopeful, I was also hesitant. They hadn't seen me yet and I had already been turned down so many times. I thought that when they would see the extent of the damage, they might change their minds. I was high risk.

Nevertheless, I was willing to have my heart broken again if need be. After all, the fella meant business after my sermon, so perhaps the hospital would mean business with me. I made the two-hour trip south to Temple and parked on campus. When I walked into the door of the hospital, I was actually *greeted* by hospital staff. It was as if I was an honored guest. This was new.

"Welcome, Mr. McRae. We're so glad to have you here. Just have a seat. Mr. Salvino has called and taken care of all the arrangements. Would you like any refreshments as you wait?"

I was dumbfounded. *Did I just walk into a regional hospital or a Sandals Resort?* Refreshments were not the norm in my experience. Had Victor told them I was some sort of royalty? It was a mystery.

As I waited to be checked in, I looked over at a huge wall display near the entrance. There were massive plaques with the names of big shot donors to the hospital. A name near the top stood out—*Victor Salvino*. The royal treatment began to add up.

When I went back for the evaluation, I handed the doctor the x-rays I previously had done. He looked them over and then up at me. He browsed over my files intently, then glanced at me again.

"Are you a Christian?" the doctor asked.

"Yes, sir, I am. I'm a pastor."

"I could tell you were a believer when you walked in the door," he told me.

"Well, I may be a pastor, but I'm a pastor in pain. Is there anything you can do?"

"We are going to do everything we can, Mr. McRae. I have hope for your case."

This was more than refreshing to hear coming from a surgeon, because at that time, I was working on borrowed hope. They wasted no time getting me in for surgery. Victor really had blazed a trail for me.

I stayed in a hotel room that night and returned the next morning for surgery. They did not put me under anesthesia for this procedure, which I initially thought was going to be a big mistake. As I was being prepped, the doctor told me he had a dream the night before, and in the dream, he was praying for me.

This was my kind of doctor.

It was by far the most refreshing and anointed experience I'd had in a medical facility. He went on mapping the surgery.

"Chris, I felt like the Lord said that we are needing to do a sweeping procedure from left to right in your torso. I believe this is going to help get your pain under control."

I thanked God for the revelation He gave to this doctor. It's one thing to have a competent doctor using expertise to repair a body. It's another thing when that doctor is partnering with the Creator Himself along the way. I was in good hands, in more ways than one. Often, when we struggle with despair, God will reveal things to others to inject us with a fresh sense of hope and inspiration. This surgery proved such.

Because the hospital was located right next to Fort Hood, the team was familiar with military injuries, gunshot wounds, and the like. I was just another day at the office for them, which is far better than having a medical team look at your injuries while scratching their heads.

I could not help but see prophetic gestures all over the scenario. I was being aided and brought to health by a *Victor*, to have my body, the *temple* of the Holy Spirit, worked on in a city called *Temple*. God, in His kindness, was leaving His fingerprints all over the place.

As the procedure was underway, the surgical team started sticking me with all kinds of needles. Because I was awake, I could hear and smell my flesh burning as they cauterized some of the offending nerve endings. Fortunately, I couldn't feel a thing.

Lo and behold, they pulled a massive bullet fragment from my body and showed it to me. *Good Lord,* I thought. *No wonder I had been in so much pain.* Throughout the procedure, I kept hearing *clink* sounds. At first, I couldn't identify what it was. Then I realized it was the noise of pieces of bullet being dropped into the pan as they were being extracted.

The staff wrapped up, stitched up, and concluded their operation. The only way to adequately describe the improvement is to say it was like a switch was flipped. I went from constant, nagging pain, to feeling relief in a matter of three days following that procedure. I was never the same again.

My hopelessness was replaced with joy. My pain was converted to relief. My weakness was made strong. The goodness of God in the midst of the journey was ever present and ever paving a way for me. The miracle began with my parents praying for me before the incident ever even occurred and that miracle is continuing to grow into maturity as the years pass.

Miracles are like trees. At first, they begin in seed form, sometimes small and not always noteworthy to human eyes. Yet in time they sprout, mature, and develop with branches growing in every direction. We look back at our lives and see so many little offshoots of the goodness of God that it's almost hard to count and track the number of times He has shown Himself on our behalf.

While I'm certainly not interested in putting myself in front of a projectile again, I can say with certainty that I have seen God work this situation for good (see Romans 8:28). The trump card of God is that He can take all of the messy, murky situations that we find ourselves in and rework them to cause a *testimony* to leap out of the *test* for all to marvel at His majesty.

CHAPTER THIRTEEN

LESIONS AND LESSONS

M y pain can become your parable. This fact really, truly is the silver lining of this horrible accident. When crisis happens and we get through it, our job is not to avoid discussing it or shove it in a box buried somewhere in our conscience. Instead, we should *lean* and *learn*. What is God saying through it? How can our *problems* actually *prophesy* to us?

King David fought many battles in his lifetime, following that early defeat of Goliath. Yet those future successes were likely fueled by the fact that he already had the cranium of a giant in his hand. His past victory may well have fueled his future ones.

Over the years, I have often considered how to

squeeze all the juice I can out of this testimony. There is no shortage of maxims, truths, and insights to be gathered. Without revisiting that Texas ranch in too much rigorous detail, I would like to return for a moment to extract some weighty wisdom from the occurrence.

––––––

First things first, there is *nothing* that causes people to make wrong turns in life quite like *anger*. Fleshly, carnal irritation has a way of crawling under our skin, grabbing the reins, and forcing us into directions we ought not be going. Wrath is like an inaccurate road sign, pointing us to places that are not in our best interest.

There are well over 100 passages in Scripture on anger, warning us against its effects. Whether it's Moses killing an Egyptian (see Exodus 2:11-22) or Michel rebuking David's exuberant worship (see 2 Samuel 6:16-23), Scripture is full of accounts warning us of anger.

Being angry with my buddy that night set the stage for me to leave where I said I would be and to go to the lake to sift through my irritation. I was in the wrong place at the wrong time, not because of some benign, careless reason—but because of *anger* itself. Anger has a way of blinding us to common sense and consequences.

Paul plainly said, "Let all bitterness, wrath, anger, clamor, and evil speaking be put away from you, with all malice. And be kind to one another, tenderhearted, forgiving one another, even as God in Christ forgave you" (Ephesians 4:31-32). Wrath is costly. It often positions us in vulnerable ways. In my case, it positioned me for a bullet. In other cases, it positions people for divorce papers, foreclosure notices, or jail cells.

God minced no words when He said that *the wages of sin are death* (see Romans 6:23). This means that sin *pays you*. Not in the form of currency. Not in the form of stocks and bonds... but in the form of death, decay, and destruction. You can earn as much of it as you want, but I don't recommend it. Anger eats away at our bottom line by destroying the very things in our lives that God wants to protect. Kindness deflects trouble, whereas anger invites it. Mine had invited trouble, to the tune of a piece of lead moving 2,300 feet per second in my direction.

That bullet was not some rough hewn, chunk of metal either. It was specifically and carefully designed to have maximum impact on its target. The enemy of your soul does not wing it. He plots, plans, and draws up blueprints for an attack on your life. When the devil wants to take out a target, he carefully designs the assault.

His projectile is the lies, threats, temptation, and deception he spews in your ear. Paul described these as *fiery darts* in Ephesians 6. The good news is that we have not been left without defense. The fiery dart may be intentionally designed, yet our shield of faith has been carefully crafted before the dart ever left the enemy's mouth. The Scripture is clear: "above all, taking the shield of faith with which you will be able to quench *all* the fiery darts of the wicked one" (Ephesians 6:16, emphasis added).

How many fiery darts does the shield quench? *All* of them. Paul used the adjective *fiery* on purpose. In ancient battle, an arrow was meant to hit, wound, and kill a target. Yet an arrow-on-fire was meant to hit a target, and then proceed to burn down anything in that area. It was the archery version of a Molotov cocktail.

When that bullet hit me, not only did it damage the target, but it set fire to other areas of life too, which would take time to extinguish and recover from. Satan does not want to merely hit you with a dart; he wants to set you and your world on fire. *This* is exactly why the shield of faith is so crucial to carry.

Paul spoke on spiritual warfare more than anyone in the Scriptures and we could learn a great deal from his insight. To the Corinthians he said, "...lest Satan should take advantage of us; for we are not ignorant of his devices" (2 Corinthians 2:11). His "devices" are the plans, schemes, and purposes for your life.

If we are *ignorant* of his devices, we will be *endangered* by his devices. The most dangerous trap is the one you do not see coming. If you see it, you can avoid it. If you recognize it, you can remove it. When God said that His people perish due to a lack of knowledge, He really meant it (see Hosea 4:6).

The picture is clear: had I been aware that I was on the receiving end of a well-formed .762 round, I would have turned on the four-wheeler and high tailed it out of there. Yet I was unaware. The bullet that was formed and fired did not prosper like it probably should have. God said in Isaiah, "No weapon formed against you shall prosper" (Isaiah 54:17). No carefully designed threat or assault shall have its way with you, as you remain aware and diligent in your faith walk.

I mentioned prior that the bullet came accompanied by a sound so loud that it's nearly beyond words. It was like having a locomotive engine blasting an inch from my ear. In your own life, some of the loudest noises you hear are from the enemy himself. He is and has always been a *noisemaker*. When he steals, kills, and destroys, he does so with volume. Noise is all he has got. In fact, the Apostle Peter instructed us to, "Be sober, be vigilant; because your adversary the devil walks about like a roaring lion, seeking whom he may devour" (I Peter 5:8).

Many scholars have long pointed to two key words in this passage: *like* and *may*. It does not say that the enemy *is* a roaring lion. It says he is *like* one. He is *all roar* with *no bite*. He will talk about his sharp teeth, without actually having any. He may boast about how he will ravage your life, without having any power to back it up. The only power he has is the power you transfer to him by believing the lie.

He does not devour whomever he wishes. He only devours those that he *may* devour. Refuse to give him the option. Become *undevourable* by standing fast in truth and rejecting the loud noise of the lie.

So often in life, the loud lie of the enemy shows up and actually *agrees* with our circumstances. Perhaps your business and marriage are failing, your personal spiritual life is a wreck, and all hope seems lost. The enemy will, with great volume, step into that situation and say, "Yep, it's all over. You're hopeless. You're lost. God has forgotten you. The church does not care. You're finished."

The lie is actually *easy* to believe because it seems to *confirm* our circumstances rather than *counter* our circumstances. Yet at the end of the day, it is God's Word that should have the final say-so. God declares that hope has been shed abroad in our hearts by the Holy Spirit (see Romans 5:5). The Lord announces we are *not* lost but found. We are not forgotten and forsaken. The curtain is not closing, God is not finished!

God elevates and exalts His Word above His own name (see Psalm 138:2). It's a staggering statement. This can only mean that we ought to elevate His Word above our situations, what we see, what we think, and what we feel. The sound of the bullet may be loud. The echo of the enemy's roar may be noisy. Yet it is an empty threat, as we cling to the promises of God.

At the end of the day, the enemy is nothing more than a chatterbox. His weapon is his word, and his ammunition is you believing it. When this whole human story is wrapped up, God gives us a glimpse into the response of those who see the enemy for what he really is. "Those who see you will gaze at you, and consider you, saying: 'Is this the man who made the earth tremble, who shook kingdoms, who made the world as a wilderness and destroyed its cities, who did not open the house of his prisoners?'" (Isaiah 14:16-17).

In other words, one day, people will look at the devil and say, "Oh my Lord... is this really the weaselly voice box that we allowed to ruin lives? Is this the tiny imp that nations were afraid of? He's nothing!" He projects himself with great volume, tells you about his teeth, when all he has are gums. His territory has been stripped away. At Calvary, he was left with no authority. Zilch. Nada. As we *turn up* the volume on the Word of God, we drown out all other voices of dissent.

————

When I reflect back on my "last words" as I lay there bleeding out, it occurs to me that many folks don't know that they are speaking their last words when they are. I had the advantage of seeing my exit on the horizon, but often, we do not. Our next breath in life is not always promised. So are we treating our words like they may be our last?

We have all heard the phrase "live like you are dying," but how many of us *truly* take it to heart? Why withhold your affection from Jesus? Why wait to push your chips to the center of the table? Your family, your friends, your workplace, your community are all waiting for you to love Him.

As we live our lives from this place of relationship with Jesus, we lead a life free from regrets and compromise. We could go at any time and know that we departed at peace with God and peace with those around us.

If anything, the incident caused me to see the fragility of life and how much we need to be sobered up by this reality. I've been pastoring for decades now and have sat with many as they approached their leap to heaven. I have *never* met someone who faced the reality of death saying, "I wish I would have made more money." I've never heard them say, "I wish I would have bought more things."

Deathbed regrets are nearly always similar in scope. "I wish I would have spent more time with my family. I wish I would have told my dad I loved him. I wish I would have spent more time getting to know my kids."

Don't wait for a funeral to send flowers and cards. Send them now. Don't hold off until a memorial service to brag on a loved one. Tell them while they're still here. My last words were not uttered on that ranch like I thought they would be. Those final words will come one day in the future. Yet between now and then, I aim to live with Christ-centered intentionality and an awareness of how life is a vapor (see James 4:14).

If you're struggling with figuring out how to live this kind of life, don't stay silent. Ask for help. Plug in with trusted mentors. After I was shot, the only relief I found was in screaming and crying out. Why? Because screaming physically helped my diaphragm push upwards, causing my spasming muscles to relax. Silence meant agony. Likewise, I am certain that some reading this may be slowly suffering and dying in silence. Perhaps you have pain, trauma, or loss in your life. You've been told to be strong and suck it up. Rub some dirt on it and move ahead.

As a result of these sentiments, we walk through life smiling on the outside but silently collapsing on the inside. We go through the motions at church, zombie our way through the workday, and never pierce the surface among our family. This underlying emotional suffering can be less obvious, but not any less traumatic than physical pain. Henry David Thoreau said, "The mass of men lead lives of quiet desperation."

When folks experience this kind of agony, they generally react in one of three ways. They either live permanently with the pain and respond to life *from* that pain, or they stuff it down so far that they don't even know it's there until years later when events trigger those buried pangs. The cliché rings true: hurting people hurt people.

To those hurting and without relief, I would encourage you to choose the third path: scream out. Don't allow silence to inflame and agitate your emotional spasming, so to speak. Some cover and mask pain with drugs, alcohol, and even seemingly benign distractions. Yet a vocal cry for help can alleviate suffering and bring a measure of help that you cannot find elsewhere.

Connect with someone in your church. Seek out a trusted leader. The body of Christ is designed to operate like our own bodies. When one part fails, the other parts do what they can to help. When I was shot, my hands instantly, instinctively went to cover the wound as my legs gave way. Every part of my being was reacting to the trauma. The body of Christ is meant to work in a similar fashion. When one is suffering, we respond to the outcry with help, love, prayer, encouragement, prophetic insight, and assistance from heaven. When one member is hurting, we all have hands on deck to help.

The problem is that the body of Christ cannot respond if a hurting sheep is holding their scream inside.

In the same way that I initially had the wind knocked out of me, unable to vocalize anything, many in the church have the wind knocked out of them. People are suffocating from the attacks on their life. They have been knocked out of the place God had them and they're scrambling just to get a breath, let alone cry out. When the world is crashing down on you, fight for your voice. Battle for your breath. When David was at an all-time low, he did not say that he would merely survive, but said, "I shall not die, but live, *and declare the works of the Lord*" (Psalm 118:17, emphasis added).

There is a declaration on the other side of your survival. There is a voice to be lifted up. There is help to be gained. In that critical hour in my life, I had help from my pastor friends. They stayed with me and prayed for me. Yet their help could only go so far. As crucial as it is to get help from the body of Christ, the body of Christ cannot be a *substitute* for your own participation in your recovery.

When the men had dropped me multiple times, it became clear that I needed to participate in helping myself. The best of friends, with the best of intentions, will not be able to get you where you need to be by themselves.

When I reflect back on my life, I see times where I needed a direct encounter with God, with no middleman. When God showed up and rattled my cage in that blue chair at age 14, God did what no man could do. When the Lord spoke to me in the car about marrying my bride, He gave me the confidence in a moment that a counselor could not in a lifetime. People can encourage you to partner with God, but they cannot *replace* your partnership with Him.

Perhaps you've felt *dropped* by people at one time or another. Maybe folks had good intentions and really wanted to help, but didn't have what it took to bring about lasting change in your life. Sometimes we feel alone as a result. The church has tried to help, the government has attempted to help, family has tried to assist, but at the end of the day, we feel like we are alone in the dirt bleeding out. That's when we've got to get up, dig our heels into the ground, and crawl our way into that truck bed, so to speak.

For a moment, I wanted to die on the ground rather than climb into the truck bed. These are the defining moments in our lives where brokenness can lead to breakthrough. When we want to throw in the towel on our marriage, our finances, or our mental health, it's high time to stand up and seek out an authentic encounter with the living God. There is something to be said for those who dig their heels in the dirt, plant their flag, and refuse to be moved.

Paul said, "...you may be able to stand your ground, and after you have done everything, to stand" (Ephesians 6:13 NIV). Sometimes the grand miracle you're experiencing is not walking on water or floating in a cloud of glory. But it's to simply *stand* when gravity is doing everything it can to push you back down.

May God Himself put a fight in us that declares, *come hell or high water, I'm in this thing to carry out what God has called me to do.* This is the posture that shakes nations and causes hell to tremble. Those who expect

God to do absolutely *everything* for them are those who have not understood the biblical model for victory. The Word states, "And the God of peace will crush Satan under *your* feet shortly" (Romans 16:20, emphasis added). If God wanted to, He would just crush the enemy under His own feet on our behalf. Yet Paul states specifically that God is indeed crushing the enemy, yet *we* are His weapon of choice. He is using *our* feet to do it.

Our participation in the process of healing and recovery is not optional. It's required. God will not do for you what He has asked you to do. He will most certainly empower and grace the process. But our will and intentions have to be engaged with the plan. The enemy would love for you to stay inactive, on the sidelines, and silently waiting for change that never comes. Yet God wants to put a fight in us to rise up and stand for our futures, our families, and our purposes.

There is a destiny that God wants to unfold in front of you, and I can promise you that it's worth fighting for. You might be at the end of your rope. Don't fear, God has more rope for you. If the grave could not hold our Jesus, then your despair cannot hold you.

While in the dirt, I was told, "You've got to get up!" It was a stark but needed warning. In Acts 12, in a prison cell, Peter was nudged on the ribs by an angel that said, "You've got to get up!" In 1 Kings 19, Elijah was at his lowest, wanting to die, when an angel said, "You've got to get up!" Perhaps God would whisper in your ear, "You've got to get up! Once you do, I'll do the rest."

Just maybe you need to touch His garment, climb that tree, or bust open that alabaster box. Maybe you should gather those five smooth stones, stretch out your withered hand, or crawl your way to the pool of Bethesda. No matter the miracle we wish to appropriate, we must step out and do what we can do, so that God can do what only He can do.

CHAPTER FOURTEEN

MESSAGES FROM THE MESS

Pain is not an enemy. It has a way of tapping you on the shoulder and informing you that something is off. If we will approach it correctly, we will see pain as a counselor, providing steps for us to get well. See, pain points to something beyond itself. If an area of our lives is throbbing, consider it a warning and a call to action. As I waited for the helicopter in that gurney, I desperately wanted something to take away my pain. Mask it, numb it, or desensitize it—I didn't care. Whatever it took, I was game. Yet, a quick fix in that moment could have been a long-term detriment to me.

Pain should direct us to seek out a diagnosis *and* a remedy from the Lord. We have all heard stories of folks who ignored pains for months or years on end, only to have it checked out when it became unbearable, at which point it was too late to treat. Imagine this same process playing out in the emotional realm. Many suppress and mask painful trauma only for it to resurface at inopportune times later in life. Suppressed pain will grow with interest, so when it surfaces again, it will be bigger and more problematic than it ever was initially.

Don't waste your pain. Press into it and grow from it. Often our pain motivates us to ask the wrong questions like, "Why me? How is this fair?" While these sentiments are definitely understandable, we ought to instead ask, "What is this pointing to? How can I partner with the Lord to remedy this?" and "What can I learn from it?" I could not magically take the bullet out of me and pretend no damage was done. But I *could* draw messages from the mess that may translate well to others who are in their own crisis.

The truth is, some have gone through things that no one else is aware of. As a result, they feel alone in the deep pain happening inside of them. The rest of the world is totally unaware of the betrayal and the hurt. At times, the hurt is someone else's doing, and other times, it's our own. Regardless, the hurt is real—but heaven has the final word. No demon in hell and no person on the planet can stop what God wants to do in your life when you are walking with Him. The *purpose* is greater than the *pain*. The *plan* is bigger than the *problem*.

Jesus said, with a straight face, "In the world you will have tribulation; but be of good cheer, I have overcome the world" (John 16:33). Not only has He overcome the tribulation we might experience, but He has overcome the entire world that presents all possible tribulation now and in the future. God did not just pass the test for you. He aced *every* test *and* got the diploma on your behalf. You don't fight to overcome. You start as an over-comer.

Why is this so important? Because these are the principles of heaven, and heaven has the final word. Roadblocks will come, surprises will jump out at you, and detours will happen, yet God has the final say-so. Learn to come into agreement with what God has spoken over you. How do we do this? Through one single six-letter word: *prayer*. If my testimony yields any fruit in your life, I want it to yield a desire for prayer.

Prayer made all of the difference in my survival and is continuing to make all of the difference in my recovery. If you are a first-generation Christian, know that you have the power to change the course of eternity for your own family and those that follow your example. You can be the one who turns to God in prayer for your loved ones and intercedes on their behalf. You are equipped with the world-changing weapon of prayer and fasting. You can find your own special refuge in God to meet daily and fight battles from your knees. Prayer is not just the difference between things going *bad* and things going *good*. It's the difference between life and death. Press into it.

If prayer is not an absolute core value in your life, you will be seriously malnourished spiritually. Make no mistake about it. God does not merely respond to *needs*. We are each a walking bag of *needs*. Yet many have needs that go unmet. Why? Because God responds to *requests*. James mentioned that we *have not* because we *ask not* (see James 4:2). Prayer is a delivery system for the benefits of God.

Often, we don't know what to pray. The Bible gives us some recourse on this. Praying in tongues is the perfect route to take in those situations (see Romans 8:26). We think we know the perfect prayer, but we often really don't. In lieu of praying in English, John prayed in tongues for me in the back of the truck. It was the perfect prayer and always is. Why? Because when we pray in tongues, we cannot miss it. We are giving God His own words back to Him.

As I and many others prayed while I was in the back of the truck on my way to rendezvous, I transitioned from speaking to God to speaking to myself at one point. If it's true that only crazy people speak to themselves, then call me loony, because I still do it to this day. In fact, it's biblical. There are times when you won't have someone to encourage you, so you begin to encourage yourself.

In 1 Samuel 30, David was in a low place, on the brink of public execution at the hands of his own people. They had some grievances with their leader, to put it mildly. They obviously were not going to provide encouragement. They were interested in hitting him with rocks, not words of affirmation. As a result, the Bible says that he *encouraged himself in the Lord*.

We've got to learn the art of encouraging ourselves. Occasionally you may need to cross over from praying for an answer to personal affirmation. Learn to change vehicles when needed, so to speak. In the midst of my emergency, I had to leap from the ground to a truck, from a truck to an ambulance, from an ambulance to a helicopter, and from a helicopter to the O.R. The road to wholeness often means we change our method. Don't be married to one particular means. Allow yourself to ebb and flow with grace.

There are times in life when one has got to realize that something that may have helped in the past is no longer of any service. On that night, the ambulance crew did all they could do for me, but their help had been exhausted. The emergency aid they could offer hit a ceiling. The helicopter blew through that ceiling and did what an ambulance could not with greater efficiency. Some of you may need to get out of the ambulance and get into a place where God can take you *higher* than you've ever been before. Let Him lift you above your trouble. He will elevate you beyond the mess in your midst.

———

Help has a sound. Relief has a way of announcing itself to you as it comes into your life. Perhaps it's the sound of a friend encouraging you. It could be the sound of a timely worship song or a doctor telling a loved one that they are in remission. Maybe it is the sound of a sigh, knowing your student loans are paid off. For me, it was the whipping blades of a helicopter. At other times, it's been the sound of my child's *I love you, Daddy,* after I've had a rough day. Regardless of the circumstances or predicament, help has a sound, and that help is coming.

For all of us, our true help sounds like nails being driven into the hands and feet of a Savior on a cross. It sounds like the humble voice of the Lord crying out, "It is finished!" It sounds like an impossibly large stone being rolled away, revealing an empty tomb. *This* is the sound of our redemptive realities.

The Bible says that faith comes from hearing the Word of God (see Romans 10:17). I've attempted to lace the Word of God throughout this book because my writing can only take you so far. My testimony is limited. The Word of God is not. The Word picks up where our earthly limitations leave off. May we be inspired, by faith, to transfer our trust to this glorious King named Jesus. I heard the helicopter before I saw it, not unlike how we hear the promises of God before we see them manifest. You may be tired, weary, in pain, and struggling from past or current trauma and drama. Perhaps your hope levels are at an all-time low and you are running on fumes. It's not over. Rock bottom might just be the rocky foundation you need to build the rest of your life on.

The enemy would love to convince you that you've received the cut-off sign. He wants you to think that God has waived His hand in front of His neck, signaling that it's over for you. The EMS workers in the helicopter certainly thought it was over for me, and here I am decades later. It's far from over. You are far from finished. Nothing you go through will be wasted.

Many people think they're finished and that the

purposes of God are unattainable. They feel they are always going to be broke and will never reach their financial dreams. They feel they will never get that promotion. That they'll never be healthy or never will see restoration in a relationship. Maybe you have fallen under a generational curse—your father was always an angry man, and you think you will be the same way. Maybe you've given your own self the cut-off signal and decided that you will never reach your goals and dreams.

When people hear something repeated enough, they eventually start to believe it. Words and thoughts have the kind of power that establishes strongholds in our thinking. When you grew up hearing that you'd *never amount to anything,* on repeat, you run the risk of buying into that notion and hampering your own explosive potential.

Perhaps we've given ourselves a self-induced cut-off sign in our lives. Living in unforgiveness is a surefire way to do so. Holding onto a grudge only serves to hold yourself back. When you hold a personal grudge, you hold your own person captive.

Whether the cut-off signal is stemming from the world, the enemy, or from our own actions, one thing is certain: it is not from God. John records the words of Jesus, telling us that the enemy comes to steal, kill, and destroy (see John 10:10). The enemy will always point to the negative and present you with pessimism. Yet the lies and threats must be countered with the rest of the passage in John 10:10 which declares that Jesus has come to give us life, *and life more abundantly.*

The abundant life is our destiny. Is this a life in which you are free from all your problems? *No.* It's simply a life in which you are free from being *destroyed* by all your problems. Paul said, "We are hard-pressed on every side, yet not crushed; we are perplexed, but not in despair; persecuted, but not forsaken; struck down, but not destroyed—always carrying about in the body the dying of the Lord Jesus, that the life of Jesus also may be manifested in our body" (2 Corinthians 4:8-10).

Notice he said, "That the life of Jesus also may be manifested in our body." The primary thrust of the gospel is incarnational—God became a man and walked among us. Now, this same God dwells in us through the Holy Spirit and enables us to carry out the works He has called us to. In good and bad, in rich and poor, in sickness and in health, we are brides of Christ with laid down lives. I encourage you, wed yourself to your purpose. Don't allow anything or anyone to derail what God has in store for you.

Speed bumps and barriers will come. Just don't stop moving. A wise man once said, "Those who do not move do not feel their own chains." Many are bound, without realizing it, because they simply have lost all forward progress.

When I look back at my life and that pivotal scene on the ranch, I see barriers that became my launchpad. I see agony that became an allegory. Everything from the sound of the blast to the sound of rescue—I see Jesus in the midst of it. The man at the site, being an attorney, acted as our advocate to dismiss the concerns of the police. Christ Himself is our advocate and defender in the midst of all of our lapses, defending us to the Father (see 1 John 2:1).

I then reflect on my desire to stay in that warm, soft hospital bed. Oh, how the enemy would love to get us to stay comfortable. The problem is that breakthrough is just outside of your comfort zone. Your promotion is just beyond that cozy setup you have going. The excuses to stay in that bed were as easy to find as water in a lake. Excuses are attracted to those critical moments.

I can't move ahead because of how I grew up; I can't step out because I didn't have a dad growing up; I can't change my lifestyle because I've been too hurt by the church; I can't be effective in the world because I lack the money. All excuses have one thing in common: self-focus. When we switch our gaze from self-focused to God-focused, we understand His mighty Spirit has been placed in us and that what we accomplish is not by power, not by might, but by His Spirit (see Zechariah 4:6).

It's time to get out of bed. It's time to take the first step. Let God disrupt your pity-party. What is it that has you down? What physical or emotional pain is keeping you from getting up? Bertha put me on notice. I was getting out of that bed that day. May God put us on notice that we are going to stand up and move ahead, regardless of anything else.

You don't have to remain a victim for the rest of your life. I may have felt like a victim for a season, but God sent a literal Victor, Victor Salvino, to connect dots and assist my medical journey. You don't have to be a prophet to see that God has sent an eternal Victor in our midst 2,000 years ago and nothing has been the same since. Not only was Jesus our victor, but He has allowed us to share in the victory also.

We are *more* than conquerors through Christ Jesus (see Romans 8:37), so get up out of that proverbial bed, stick your leg out, and take a step. Then go for another after that. Lay back down if you must, but tomorrow, get back up again. Refuse to complain about the place you are in and start thanking God that He has gone before you, and that there's breath in your lungs. Thank Him that you have the privilege of waking up in the morning, to rejoice and be glad in it. These are not words of hollow encouragement or mere positive confession. This is the power of God.

This is more than *faking it 'til you make it.* It's not an external exercise in looking strong and spiritual. No, it's much deeper than that. In the same way that my wound was left open to heal from the inside out, God wants to mend us from the inside out. Jesus called the Pharisees "white-washed tombs" because they looked good on the outside, but inside they were *dead.*

We live in a time where everyone seems to be worried about what things look like on the outside. We spend so much time on behavior modification and presentation. We want to do things right, but God says that in order to get it right on the outside, we start with the inside. Sanctification is an inside job. He plunges into the depths of our hearts and clears the skeletons from our closets. This great physician leaves nothing untouched, and this healing is far more than physical. Christ's stripes brought about healing in every sphere of our lives. Nothing is exempt.

May the Holy Spirit vacuum out the infections that have grown in our souls. May foreign matter begin to surface in our hearts and minds and be removed accordingly. Everything we see in the natural is like a type and shadow of the spiritual. Our spirits work similarly to our bodies. For example, the fragments in my body were pushing their way to the surface by design. The body recognizes an intruder and forces it out. Likewise, our spirits are aware of things that are not supposed to be there.

Things like fear and anxiety are good examples of foreign matter that lie beneath the surface and attempt to take up residence in us. Yet our spirits and souls were not meant to carry these things. As a result, we will begin to reject and push back against these fragments. Anger is another type of foreign matter that will keep us in pain and darkness if we don't allow it to be removed.

Envy, lust, dishonesty, cowardice, pride, and the like are all pieces of shrapnel caused by the fall of man. For ages, people attempted to remove them but could not. Our hearts and minds rejected these things deep down, but we had no way to get rid of them—until Jesus came as a Master Physician, removing the unwanted fallout of Adam's disobedience.

Our prayer should be, "God, I do not want *anything* in me that You did not put there." Some foreign fragments will work their way out in the flow of the Christian life without too much discomfort. Others need to be carefully, intentionally, and surgically removed by God. We've all had habits and issues that were easy to drop and didn't give it a second thought. Then we've had those nagging issues that needed daily repentance and deliverance. No matter the situation, great or grim, God wants to work His way and bring you into the fullness of Christ.

———

As I button up this raw testimony, one thing that comes to mind is the simple reality that the very thing that was meant for my harm ended up working together for my good. Of course, my friends on the retreat did not mean harm to me, but the unforgiving bullet was certainly made for harm. Despite all of that, God has crafted a story and an experience that has produced more fruit than I could have imagined. It brings to mind the life of Joseph.

Joseph was the eleventh-born son of Jacob. Jacob loved him more than he loved his other sons and even gifted him with a snazzy, multi-colored coat. This of course infuriated his brothers as they steamed with envy. In fact, they were so eaten up by jealousy that they sold Joseph into slavery.

Upon his arrival in Egypt, he was assigned to a leader named Potiphar. As dire as the circumstances might have seemed, God was relentlessly coming to Joseph's aid. It seemed as though his newfound favor could not be interrupted. That is, until Potiphar's wife tried to seduce him. When Joseph did not reciprocate her feelings and fled the situation, she later lied about Joseph's actions and had him thrown in prison.

Consider this: every time it seemed like Joseph experienced favor, the enemy came in and made things worse. But the story doesn't end there. While in prison, Joseph became known for being able to interpret dreams. Word got out to government officials and Joseph received yet another promotion. King Pharaoh called on him to interpret a couple of dreams that he himself did not understand. God enabled Joseph to interpret those dreams and to save Egypt from a severe famine. The Pharaoh appointed Joseph as second in command.

To think, Joseph went from *slave*, to *prisoner*, to *second in command to the King* is incredible as is. Somehow, the story gets even better. The famine had spread throughout surrounding lands, in particular, the land where Joseph's family originated. The brothers who had sold Joseph had caught wind that there was grain available in Egypt and set out to go buy some.

When they arrived, they did not recognize Joseph as their brother, but Joseph recognized them. Through a series of requests, Joseph tested the integrity of his brothers. They passed the test and Joseph revealed his identity to his family. As one might imagine, they were terribly sorry and begged for forgiveness. Joseph responded, "But as for you, you meant evil against me; but God meant it for good, in order to bring it about as it is this day, to save many people" (Genesis 50:20).

Joseph recognized that his life, with all of the unthinkable twists and turns, even when it seemed that all was lost, was not a shot in the dark. No matter his circumstances and ups and downs, God continued to promote and favor him, ultimately working the worst of scenarios for Joseph's good.

My life, with all of the wild twists and turns, ups and downs, is also not a shot in the dark. God has used every bit of my story, all of the problems, and all of the pain to bring glory to Himself. He may not have *caused* all my trouble, but He will *work* all my trouble for good.

You may find yourself in a good place, like you've just been given a multi-colored coat, so to speak. Rest assured, trouble will come. You may find yourself in a bad place, like you've just been sold into slavery. Rest assured, promotion will come. No matter your current state, good or bad, the overarching goal of the gospel is to bring *abundant life* to fruition in your life.

Perhaps you feel as though the enemy is winning, and winning big. Be assured that this is short-lived as you lean into Jesus. You will not stay behind bars. Defeat is not your inheritance. Death is not your portion. From the prison to the palace, God has got you. Your circumstances are bound to change by the God who takes interest in your plight. Let Him step in and change the narrative of your story.

So often we allow the ups and downs of life to determine what we believe, and what we do not believe, about ourselves and God. This misguided mode of thinking has cost so many, so much. We don't accrue our doctrine based on whether or not we are in the hospital or whether or not we are in pain. We believe what we believe about God and ourselves through His Word. *Nothing more, nothing less, and nothing else.*

So it begs the question, what *does* the Word say?

The Word is clear that you are not here by accident (see Jeremiah 1:5). You may *make* mistakes—that does not mean you *are* one. You might *experience* failure—that does not mean you *are* a failure. You are not what you do, you are *who* God says you are. Your life is not a shot in the dark. It's not an aimless projectile floating through life. God has released you with a destiny that's bound to be fulfilled and not wasted, as you bind yourself to His blueprints and partner with His plan.

CHAPTER FIFTEEN

THE FALLOUT AND THE FUTURE

Lifelong hunters don't hang up their rifles and quit the sport easily, but I did. I was happy to live the remainder of my days without another animal in my crosshairs. Something about nearly dying on a hunt has a way of ruining your appetite for the chase. So I gave it up. My lifelong passion was no longer going to be *lifelong*. That is, until a conversation with Pastor Terry.

See, mentors are great. They speak into your life, provide sound wisdom, and live lives worth emulating. Yet a spiritual father is *more* than a mentor. Their words and wisdom are weightier. Their care is more felt and thorough. Their insight is more personal. Their advice is more intentional. When they speak, you listen.

"Before any fear of hunting sets in and takes root, you need to get back out there and go on a hunt with me."

I was hesitant. Nervous, even. But I went.

The dry Texas ground looked better without blood puddles. The sound of distant birds was more pleasant than my own screaming. Riding inside the truck sure beat laying in the back of it. It wound up being remarkably liberating.

It was a declaration to heaven, hell, and the earth, that I was not going to be dominated by fear and angst for the rest of my life. The taxidermy I've curated for my wall since then is proof of that. It's been almost twenty years since the night I was shot. Between then and now, I've taken somewhere around 160 million breaths that I thought I never would. God's faithfulness to preserve His people for His purpose is something I'll never take lightly.

When I was finally able to return to work after a solid 6 months of intensive therapy and recovery, I was pastoring the junior high youth and loving the flow and feel of ministry work again. As I grew in life and in ministry, I had to learn to lead. On the home front, I had 4 mouths to feed and an example to set. The kids had loved having me at home all the time during my recovery. It was really hard on them when I went back to work, but eventually everything normalized.

Vanessa and I learned as we went, found our core values in the home, and worked at raising our kids in a Christ-centered environment. We learned to borrow elements of each of our upbringings. For example, our kids memorized the book of James and were taught the Word. However, it has not been as strict and rigorous as my upbringing. I wanted them to *love* the Word. When Bible reading is *bliss* and not just a *burden,* it unleashes a different measure of power in your life.

On the ministry end of things, I began to discover the value of team building. Ministry has never been a one man show. If you reduce an organization to one man with a microphone, that ministry will not go far. I started constructing my team of youth leaders, mobilizing them, and encouraging them along the way. When leading a youth event, for example, you aren't just thinking about your three points and a poem from the pulpit. You're thinking about who's going to deliver the pizza and who is picking up the plastic cups. Delegating details became essential.

They say that your team does not care how much you know until they know how much you care. I had plenty of shortcomings in those early years of ministry, but I did work to check on my leaders. I allowed them to make mistakes. I was not overly concerned with perfection or my own unique vision of things. At the same time, I occasionally had to light fires and motivate the crew.

My steady example of how to lead leaders was Pastor Terry. He would regularly check on me with inquiries like, "How's your family and marriage? How is your soul? How is your time with the Lord? Are you setting time aside for your wife? What about your kids?"

The priorities had always been clear: time with the

Lord, time with the wife, time with kids, and time in ministry—in that order. It was impressed upon me that if *I* was healthy, my ministry would be also. Knowing the value of these pastoral checkups, I would do the same thing with my leaders.

Pastor Terry helped me to grow as a more well-rounded man of God. "What are you preaching?" or "What's on your heart for the youth?" were his way of taking the spiritual temperature of the ministry. It was invaluable.

As years passed, I eventually took the high school youth pastor position. With a slightly better attention span and the ability to handle weightier topics, pastoring the high schoolers served to prepare me even more for my eventual roles in the church. Youth ministry was where I really cut my teeth preaching.

Someone said to me during that time, "Don't think you're there just to pacify these kids. *Pour in.*"

I really developed as a communicator in those years. Youth Pastor is the only job in the church where you have to do *everything*. You are handling strategy, planning, event organization, worship, preaching, follow up, discipleship. It's essentially a mini church within the church. I loved the role and savored the growth that came through it.

On more than one occasion, opportunities would come up to take different positions or to move all together. I would go to Terry about it every time. Sometimes, the offers were tempting with sweet locations, positions, and salaries. I desperately wanted him to say, "No, Chris, don't take that other position at that other church. We need you here." But he never did. That frustrated me, in a sense, because I wanted the decision to be made for me. He would instead ask, "What is God saying?"

It required me to go to Jesus directly. That process forged me into a man who would take his inquiries to the throne and get a word for myself. Terry was not interested in his own motives or convenience. He was interested in the will of God. He taught me to look at the bigger picture and see the expanded view of things. He has incorporated his business background into the ministry with such grace and ease. I always felt that if he was in my corner, I would be just fine, and still do. We were meeting weekly in those days, and the grains of insight I picked up have quite literally built my present-day ministry.

At times, I've been on the brink of making certain decisions and gone to Terry and asked, "Have you been down that road before?"

"Yeah, I have. And I personally wouldn't do it again."

He was never forceful. Always thoughtful and somewhat laissez-faire in his leadership style. He gave me a lot of rope. Did I occasionally hang myself with it? Sure. But it was a far better alternative than micromanagement in his mind. The training wheels he afforded me in those days made all the difference in my long-term success.

In the midst of my 30s, the family was maturing and my heart for the church was growing. I knew I would not pastor the youth until I was 80, but I also was not quite sure what the next season would hold. That was when the executive pastor position came available, and I was a natural fit. At one point or another, I had filled about every role in the church except bookkeeper. I knew the ins and outs of the local gathering and so moving into this role felt seamless.

I would be helping Terry run the church ministry and lead the staff, while Ronna Keller would oversee the business end of things. This also meant more pulpit time, preaching, and leading services.

I absolutely loved the executive role. I had ample time with Terry. He was like a driving instructor. I was allowed to steer and hit the gas, while still being subject to the voice in the passenger seat. One year, when he asked if I wanted to preach on Easter Sunday, I knew I was entering new realms of responsibility.

Between raising teenagers and helping run the church, my plate was full. Yet I still found room for another side dish: *further education*. I enrolled in King's University and knocked out a Christian Ministry Degree over the course of time. I picked up a class here and a class there, eventually walking the stage and collecting a diploma on May 4th of 2017. I was stretched in that season, but sometimes stretching is God's preferred method for increasing your capacity. My old wineskins were not cutting it.

The theological training was rich. The education didn't necessarily change *what* I believed doctrinally, but helped me peer into the origins of *why* I believe it. The lectures were not just solid topical sermons, but deep exposition and insight into the Scriptures. The training was not a stepping stone, but a cornerstone upon which I could continue to build.

————

Danny Silk said, "Everybody loves transition until it happens to you." Transition is great in theory, but not always fun in practice. 2019 was not touted to be a year of transition initially. It seemed that I would be in my role, Terry would be in his, and we would continue to press on faithfully. Other than plans to pursue a doctorate eventually, I didn't have a grand vision on the horizon. It was one foot in front of the other.

Thinking he would be lead pastor of Sojourn for several years to come, Pastor Terry had not formulated a comprehensive succession plan. The thought of it was spurred when his brother had retired from a long career in the travel industry. While attending a ceremony, where his brother was inducted into the travel industry hall of fame, he sat at a table with a bunch of folks who had *transitioned*. They were businesspeople who had either just executed a succession plan or were in the process of it. A seed was planted. Wheels began turning.

In the fall of that year, on a trip to California for a Bill Johnson meeting, God spoke to Pastor Terry, seemingly out of the blue, and expressed that it was, indeed, time to transition. As easy going as ever, he had no issue, rubs nor rebuttal. Others had been considered for the role, but ultimately, I was best suited for the position.

The offer surprised me a bit. It was given at lunch one day when Pastor Terry asked, "Chris, would you like to be considered for the lead pastor position?"

I considered it and chewed on the implications of the offer. I was humbled but had one single reservation.

"If you are going to ride off into the sunset and be out of here, I don't want it. If we are here together like father and son and you help me with the transition, then I am in."

I didn't just *want* Pastor Terry to stick around, but I *needed* him to be there. I sought after his guidance and help. Had he made plans to leave the area and leave the church to a new pastor without his guidance, I would have been in Florida pastoring on the beach somewhere right now, but that wasn't the case. He would be staying.

He said to me, "You catch them, I'll clean them."

As senior pastor with an evangelistic edge, I would be preaching Sunday mornings and leading the church, winning souls. Pastor Terry would still teach alongside me on Wednesdays and help to build a training platform to integrate new believers into this wonderful Christian life.

With manuals, small books, and curriculums for adults and children alike, we charted a course to operate *together* in this wild thing called ministry. January of 2020 marked the start of Sojourn Church's 33rd year in existence and my first year as Senior Pastor.

In a traditional denominational church, when a new pastor takes over, the senior leader has to leave.

Here at Sojourn, it was about family. Just because a kid grows up doesn't mean you have to leave them. The God-model is that He is the God of Abraham, Isaac, and Jacob—the God of the generations. Never for a moment have I felt like my neck was being breathed down or that I was awkwardly trying to find my place as senior pastor while Terry watched. He has been interested in one thing: humbly walking out the will of God. With a revelation that we are stewards and not owners, competition has been the furthest thing from our church culture.

It went without saying. A spiritual father is a special assignment—and I can't imagine life without Pastor Terry and my own father in particular. Without the heart of fathers and mothers in your life, you will be spiritually and relationally malnourished. The role of these figures from birth to present in my life cannot be overstated.

If you are a woman, find a God-fearing female who will walk through life alongside you. If you're a man, find a Christ-loving man of faith who will lock arms with God's purposes for your life. Spiritual parents will celebrate your victories, talk you off the ledge, keep you grounded, stand with you, pray with and for you, and point you to Jesus through it all. I know without a shadow of a doubt that Terry is *for me*, never against me. He is not trying to get anything *from* me. He also has not tried to make me like him or push me to fit a certain mold other than what God has for me.

During the transition, there can be no doubt that

this new mantle has bonded me even tighter to the body of Christ. I long to see the church as a whole truly *be* the church to the unchurched. So often we've gotten evangelism wrong by viewing salvation as a rescue mission or quick ticket to heaven. We've been set back years because we've divorced discipleship from evangelism. We have abdicated our role and let government do what the church should be doing.

Jesus referred to His message as *the gospel of the Kingdom*. The King's domain ought to supplant our domain. This means the gospel is meant to have *impact* in every sphere and level of society, from Main Street to Wall Street, blue collar to white collar, the inner city, suburbs, and rural towns alike.

Salvation itself is a surrender to the King and His rule. We don't make Him Lord of our lives. He is Lord regardless. We are called to humbly submit ourselves to His Spirit *and* His Word. On more than one occasion, I've seen believers neglect the Word in favor of the Spirit, yet the Word is our *foundation*. The Bible is our introduction to the Father. The whole book is an *about the author* section. As we submit to Him and His Word, we will find ourselves effortlessly plugging in with a local community of believers and reaping the benefits of a surrendered life.

I long to see our church, and the greater church, become a greenhouse for growth. Church is not a country club. It is a hub for increase at every point in life. We obviously cannot force people to grow, but we can create an environment that makes it more attainable. The church is a meeting point between God and man. It's a place for people to step into the reality that they are not orphans, but sons and daughters.

We, as God's people, are not short on destiny. But we are often short on an *awareness* of that destiny. We sometimes allow the wind and waves of life to eclipse our vision of that ultimate purpose. Whether that's a job loss, a hunting accident, the loss of a loved one, or a business failure, life has a way of interrupting our course. Know in the midst of the disruptions and disturbances that your life is not a shot in the dark. It's not an accident. The furthest thing from it. Your life has been intentionally, lovingly propelled and guided by the God who does not miss His target.

A NOTE ON TRAUMA

There can be no doubt, small things can have a *big* impact. Be it viruses, microchips, bullets, pacemakers, or small deeds, it's the little things that drive our world. Paul said, "a little leaven leavens the whole lump" (Galatians 5:9). Leaven is a tiny, living, expanding organism. It is *alive*. What was Paul suggesting here? That just a small amount of *life* can be the change-agent needed to alter *everything*.

Yet in the same way that God wants small things to make big impact, the enemy would like to introduce this same reality in your life, as well. So often, it's the splinters, so to speak, that find their way under our skin, and if left unchecked, can fester and cost us greatly in the long haul.

Free Indeed is a resource we provide through Sojourn Church that has born much fruit in many lives. It's a class designed to weed out old patterns, pour in new life, and bring people into total liberty through the power of the gospel. Having said that, I would be remiss if I didn't mention the value of freedom in these areas of your life. I feel the best way to land this plane is by ensuring that those who relate to my trauma have a clear path for freedom presented also.

No one would argue that getting shot is a traumatic event. Yet trauma is not reserved for hunting accidents, war veterans, and abuse victims. It's common when talking about trauma to only conjure up images of horrific incidents, but a traumatic event can be anything that one finds deeply distressing that overwhelms coping abilities. Whether you've gone through a divorce, lost a loved one, been abandoned, mistreated, or betrayed, you've likely experienced trauma in your life.

This emotional response called trauma is not only spiritual but can be physical. Be it flashbacks, nightmares, or even physical reactions like headaches and fatigue, God has a solution in the gospel. You may be all too familiar with the voice of trauma, disappointment, and despair, yet God has a new voice to introduce you to—His own.

Lean in and learn from His Word. Adjust the focus of your heart, moving it from circumstances to the God who is *over your circumstances*. Find a mentor who can identify areas of trauma and stand with you to see it broken off your life, the same way Pastor Terry did with me.

So often, we cope with trauma by simply living with

it. It lies under the surface, festering, growing, and occasionally rearing its ugly head. This unchecked trauma manifests with bitterness, discouragement, and unforgiveness. The mold that continues to grow and cause damage is the mold that is beneath the walls, not exposed to light. As we expose our internal pain to the Lord, He reveals His healing grace to us. So often we rationalize our responses by saying, "It's not fair that I went through what I went through. I have the right to cope in whatever way I want!"

What you went through may not have been the will of God and you may have had no control over the situation. Yet in that same breath, staying in that place of pain is not the will of God for you either. Unlike the initial trauma, we have the choice as to whether or not we stay in that place. If I make a wrong turn while driving, my GPS does not chew me out and call me dumb. What does it say?

"Recalculating."

God Himself is recalculating us. He is not condemning us and throwing guilt trips our way. He is not wagging His finger in our faces and pointing to our wrong turn. He simply gets us back on course.

Learn to get back on course with the Lord. Take authority over that point of pain. Tell Satan that he has no hold over you because God has paid the price for you to walk in freedom. You might have to do this weekly, daily, or even hourly until trauma loses its grip on your soul. Turn your attention to Jesus and let Him remove the stress and fear from you. He wants to take the pit in your stomach away. Replace the lie of the enemy with truth. Hold fast to the promises of God. You aren't stuck in a bad mental state, you are planted in the promises of God.

You are accepted, loved, and highly favored. As you continue to press into Him, He will cover you, change you, shape you, mold you, bless you, and transform you. Pretty soon, your gown will tie in the front, so to speak. You will be the one doing the ministry, not just receiving it. You will be the one to help others experience the same kind of freedom and healing that came to you also.

We became orphans and victims via the fall of man, but have transformed into children of God and victors through the rise of man, when Jesus walked out of the tomb. Don't allow the enemy to sell you short. God is the author and finisher of your faith. Until He punctuates the last line of your life, stay in it.

I would like to encourage you to pray this simple prayer of surrender, as you believe it in your heart:

Father God, this day, I surrender all to You. My pain, my trauma, my losses, my wins, my good, and my bad, I give it all to You. Today, I put my faith and trust in Jesus Christ and His resurrection. Help me to never be the same as I lean into Your promise. No matter what I've seen or what I have been through, You are faithful to work it all together for my good, in Jesus' name, amen.

CHRIS McRAE joined the Sojourn Staff in 1996 while attending Christ for the Nations. After Nations. He obtained an undergraduate degree from King's University and is pursuing a Master's in Theology from Southeastern University in Lakeland, Florida.

Chris is passionate about impacting the lives of families with the life changing truth from the word of God. Chris and Vanessa have been married since 1998 and have four children.

Endnotes

1. Culbertson, Howard. *At What Age Do Americans Become Christian?*, http://home.snu.edu/~hculbert/ages.htm.
2. "Feral Hogs in Texas – Management and Trapping Techniques." *Texas A&M AgriLife Extension Service*, 7 Feb. 2022, https://tinyurl.com/ypeazcwt.

For information on bulk ordering this title
at wholesale rates please visit:
TALLPINEBOOKS.COM